SHAKESPEARE'S

MEDIATED

WORLD

University of Massachusetts Press
Amherst 1976

Shakespeare's Mediated World

RICHARD FLY

Publication of this book was assisted by the
American Council of Learned Societies under
a grant from the Andrew W. Mellon Foundation.

Library of Congress Cataloging in Publication Data
Fly, Richard, 1934–
   Shakespeare's mediated world.
   Bibliography: p.
   Includes index.
   1. Shakespeare, William, 1564–1616—Criticism and
interpretation. 2. Mediation in literature. I. Title.
PR 2976.F5   822.3'3   74-32486
ISBN 0-87023-199-5

Contents

Acknowledgments

My work on this book was substantially aided by two consecutive summer grants from The Research Foundation of the State University of New York, for which I am grateful. I am also obliged to Arthur F. Kinney of the *English Literary Renaissance,* Harry R. Garvin of the *Bucknell Review,* and Ernest J. Lovell of *Texas Studies in Literature and Language* and the University of Texas Press for permission to reprint revised and conflated versions of essays that first appeared in their journals: " 'I cannot come to Cressid but by Pandar': Mediation in the Theme and Structure of *Troilus and Cressida,*" ELR, 3 (Winter, 1973), "Revelations of Darkness: the Language of Silence in *King Lear,*" BUR, 20 (Winter, 1972), and "Beyond Extremity: A Reading of *King Lear,*" TSLL, 16 (Spring, 1974).

At moments of stalemate, discouragement, or just plain lethargy, I have been aroused and urged on by teachers, colleagues, and friends. Professor Norman Rabkin's generous instruction and example gave me whatever critical discipline I possess, and it is a pleasure to acknowledge my long-standing debt to him. My friends Carl Dennis and Joe Riddel read portions of the manuscript and, in every instance, brought light and lucidity where once obscurity reigned. James L. Calderwood read the manuscript at a late stage, bringing his intelligent scrutiny to bear on virtually every page. Ed Dryden,

Fred See, and Roy Roussel, my colleagues at the State University of New York at Buffalo, made criticism possible by the sanity and wit of their company. Finally, I am especially pleased to acknowledge the help of Professor Arthur F. Kinney, the editor of *English Literary Renaissance,* whose activity on behalf of this book has gone far beyond professional courtesy.

All the quotations from Shakespeare's plays and poems are taken from *William Shakespeare: The Complete Works,* General Editor Alfred Harbage (Baltimore: Penguin Books, 1969). This edition is generally known as The Pelican Shakespeare.

Introduction

This book is primarily a study of five Shakespearean plays that have proven especially difficult for both the critic and the general audience. For the most part I concentrate on the specific qualities of each play and try to avoid blurring the great differences, generic and otherwise, between them. I bring these particular plays together for general scrutiny, however, because I believe they do share some crucial features and also because I think they offer, when studied in sequence, a more precise understanding of Shakespeare's ceaseless, ever deepening engagement with his challenging medium.

Two of the plays I discuss, *Troilus and Cressida* and *Measure for Measure,* display formal and thematic peculiarities that have caused some critics to group them together under the question-begging rubric of "Problem Plays." A third play, *Timon of Athens,* has failed to command enough critical respect to merit consideration even as a problem. Instead, commentators have usually labelled it unfinished and simply dismissed it as uninteresting to all but perhaps the textual scholar. On the other hand, *Romeo and Juliet* and *King Lear,* the other two plays I examine, are long-established masterpieces that probably measure, by their obvious differences in vision and structure, the unparalleled scope of Shakespeare's versatility in the tragic mode. Despite such sustained popularity, however, commentators continue to experience some difficulty acknowledging Shakespeare's achievement here without also admitting to certain reservations regarding the two plays' overall success as finished works of poetic drama. As in *Troilus, Measure,* and *Timon*—although to a less damaging degree—there is present in that response to *Romeo* and *Lear* an uneasy feeling that the playwright has somehow not properly gauged the creative potential of his craft nor accepted its inherent limitations. Of these different plays, in fact, only *King Lear* enjoys anything like a consistently high critical rating, and it too is not without its share of detractors.

While judgments of the quality of these plays vary widely, all five seem to respond in their peculiar forms to Shakespeare's repeated encounters with a medium that he perceives as capable, on occasion, of resisting his creative aspirations. Indeed, in those plays his artistic deployment of language and action often seems to function more to debilitate and distort communication and design than satisfactorily to fulfill them. That deployment adversely affects not only actions occurring within the plays but their rising structures as well. Hence, the characters' efforts to "suit the action to the word, the word to the action" extend to the playwright himself, making us aware of his own personal struggle for mastery. What attracts me to these troublesome plays is their common ability to elicit disturbing questions concerning Shakespeare's sense of his chosen medium's adequacy to sustain the creative ambitions he brings to it. What finally unites the discussions of the individual plays is my wish to understand and articulate the various but related ways Shakespeare dramatizes his ongoing encounter with the divisive tendencies of poetic drama.

My method, then, is to study the five plays at the most fundamental level of the creative enterprise. My subject is Shakespeare's confrontation with his medium, and my thesis, simply stated, is that certain of his plays arise out of a growing conviction—expressed in varying degrees of intensity—that poetic drama, although wide reaching, is not always answerable either to the complexities of human existence or to the art that tries to mirror it. If occasionally his plays fail to satisfy our expectations, it may be because they are about the artist's inability to create a meaningful order out of hostile and intractable materials—a general sense of failure that encompasses both their substance and structure. However, I feel these seemingly flawed plays are of great importance to Shakespeare's development because of the self-consciousness with which he perceives the problematic relationship of the artist to his medium and labors to arrive at a fuller understanding and control over it. Even *Troilus* and *Timon* do not collapse into thematic and structural incoherence because of the paradoxical lucidity with which Shakespeare finds means to use language and action to image forth not only the characters' difficulties with their hazardous environment but also his own problems with his unruly materials. Indeed, it is probably his bold willingness to explore the disjunctive propensities of his medium in plays like *Romeo* and *Measure* that makes possible the magnificent orchestrations of language and action in his more unqualifiedly successful plays. In its brilliant thematic development of the acknowledged limitations of poetic drama, *King Lear,* for instance, owes much of its expressive power to insights Shakespeare gleaned from such earlier experimentations with his medium.

The metadramatic aspects of Shakespeare's involvement with his medium are not immediately apparent in these plays. As a motif in their thematic organization the term medium merely refers to the middle or something intermediate and usually suggests the general idea of "between-ness." In my analyses of dramatic action I frequently use the term rather broadly to refer to whatever lies between the initial apprehension of some desirable goal or design and the actual realization of it. Such awareness may be shared by the characters, the playwright, and even the audience, since sensitivity to the medium will naturally increase whenever attention is deflected away from an untroubled contemplation of an end product and is engaged instead by the intervening dynamics of the process required to reach that goal. Recognition of an interfering medium will gradually arise in proportion to the capacity of the mediating process to retard anticipated satisfaction. Shakespeare can throw heavy emphasis on that kind of obstruction in several ways, but he does so most obviously by creating characters who have a natural genius for retardation. For instance, figures like Juliet's Nurse, Mercutio, Pandarus, Pompey Bum, and Apemantus seem to inhabit a world of almost pure process uninformed by any teleological sense of purpose or direction. However, their behavior gives rise to a subtle commentary on playwriting since, in their comic interactions with the more seriously engaged characters, they graphically illustrate—primarily through their directionless verbosity —how a medium can obstruct and debase desires as well as fulfill them. The prominence and centrality of these grotesque figures combine with other formal characteristics to hint strongly at an eventual frustration of all expectations, not only for the plays' deeply committed participants but for the plays themselves.

It follows that the obstructing properties latent in the concept of medium can be intensified until they begin to appear demonic and negating in their almost Manichean hostility towards all forms of human desire. At such moments the term medium may take on an exclusively tragic resonance and begin to express the felt presence of malign forces actively intervening between will and execution: material or psychic agencies that seem to interpose their mysterious resistance between inspiration and consequence. Again, both playwright and characters may share this gloomy sense of subjection to medium. For example, Shakespeare repeatedly sounds such a despairing note in *Troilus and Cressida,* where all the characters come finally to acquiesce in General Agamemnon's pessimistic conviction that no action initiated in his chaotic world will finally answer "the aim / And that unbodied figure of the thought / That gave't surmisèd shape" (I. iii. 15–17). Lovers, warriors, schemers, and artists all experience the way in which "Checks and disasters / Grow in the veins of actions highest reared" (5–6). Similarly, Romeo and Juliet seem half aware from the outset that all efforts on their behalf to "incorporate two in one" (II. vi. 37) have no real chance for success in the alien and destructive world they inhabit. And both Lear and Timon move through stages of deepening frustration until they too ultimately find in death their longed-for release from an increasingly perverse and intolerable existence. Indeed, Timon's death cry of "nothing brings me all things" (V. i. 186) voices his liberation from a life-medium conceived as totally unresponsive to desire. The sense of human possibilities is only slightly less dismal in *Measure for Measure,* although in this instance Shakespeare dramatizes his dark vision more indirectly. A fundamental inadequacy permeates the atmosphere of all these play-worlds, and that inadequacy reflects, I think, more than just the struggles of fictional characters.

Shakespeare communicates his concern with a limiting medium most directly through the comically maladroit words and deeds of carefully positioned middlemen, who function both as agents in the action and as surrogates for the playwright. The ludicrously ineffective activities of these various mediators not only define the hopelessly narrow limits of purposive human action within their plays, but also allow Shakespeare to comment tacitly on his own artistic development. In other words, the concept of medium does not remain abstract and theoretical but assumes a palpable dramatic life of its own: a corporeality that allows for a dynamic participation in the unfolding action. Perhaps the clearest example of this procedure is Pandarus, for, despite his lively image, he functions in *Troilus and Cressida* as little more than a dramatic embodiment of mediation and the related aspects of instrumentation implied by that concept. In all cases we recognize him, and the characters treat him, as an essentially indispensable middle term that actively mediates between stalemated parties. Pandarus is quite literally a central figure in *Troilus* in that his bustling creaturality and his urge to stage-manage affairs serve effectively to body forth the play's obsession with processes of flawed mediation. No explanation of the play's meaning and form can afford to neglect his role, since it is almost impossible to understand Troilus' and Cressida's love affair and its subsequent collapse without relating their experience directly to Pandarus' glaring shortcomings as their intermediary. Whatever fulfillment is available in their world is partially gauged beforehand by the discouraging capabilities of this vulgar go-between. As their linked pledges in Act III strongly imply, they are—and forever will remain—an indissoluble trio.

As mediator and surrogate playwright Pandarus belongs to a group that includes characters as diverse as Friar Laurence and Edgar. My analysis focuses attention on character groupings in which special emphasis falls on the symbolically important activities of agents because I believe that atomistic character studies of figures like Troilus and Cressida, Romeo and Juliet, and Lear and Cordelia are generally misleading, since they tend to deflect attention away from what is vitally central to their tragic experiences. Hence, my study of *Troilus and Cressida* considers the role of Pandarus—and other sub-mediators like Ulysses, Paris, and Patroclus—in an effort to better understand not only the play's disturbing vision of general collapse but also its strange and disappointing structure. *Romeo and Juliet* has an unusually rich supply of mediators, but they all seem to perform variations on a common tragic theme of hazardous arbitration. Benvolio, Romeo, Prince Escalus, the Nurse, and, most fatally, Friar Laurence, all share a damaging ineptness as mediators. The peculiarly ironic quality of the lovers' plight stems from the melancholy fact that all their intermediaries suffer increasingly bloody reversals as they attempt to carry out their good intentions. In *Measure for Measure* Shakespeare's ongoing concern with processes of flawed mediation comes to peak intensity most clearly in Duke Vincentio's sudden intervention into the hopelessly entangled lives of Isabella, Claudio, and Angelo. As a benign mediator the Duke-Friar may seem a puzzling amalgam of Friar Laurence and Pandarus, and new insight into the theme and structure of this difficult play becomes available when we view his massive and damaging intrusion into the play's action against the background of failed and perverted mediation in *Romeo* and *Troilus*.

King Lear's awesomely protracted suffering unfolds as the direct consequence of the rash autocrat's attempt to banish from his kingdom all
forms of between-ness. The royal command to "Come not between the
dragon and his wrath" (I. i. 122), although fraught with unforeseeable
ills, suggests that Shakespeare is attempting to turn away from the
densely mediated worlds of the previous plays. And indeed, the most
striking peculiarity of *Timon of Athens* is its obstinate refusal to
admit *any* operative form of the mediate into its starkly polarized
play-world. Both the protagonist and the playwright appear to share a
hatred for "the middle of humanity," and so the only mediator now
present in the action is the totally helpless and insignificant Flavius,
Timon's abandoned steward. From the richly mediated society of
Romeo to the harsh unmediated world of *Timon* stretches the area of
bold experimentation and struggle with medium on Shakespeare's part
that is the subject of this study.

Of the several kinds of mediators who operate in the plays
we can often distinguish two quite different types, who interact
dynamically with each other in a single developing action, and in the
dialectic created by this interaction Shakespeare most clearly dramatizes
his sensitivity to his medium's disjunctive proclivities. In other words,
he occasionally arranges for poetic drama to decompose into the
simpler components of language and action, and then embodies those
separated constituents in two disjunct but related dramatic agents. I
do not wish to be crudely schematic about such a delicate procedure,
but it does seem demonstrable that in *Romeo and Juliet,* for example,
Juliet's loquacious Nurse personifies medium primarily in its aspect
as language, while Friar Laurence typifies medium in its aspect as
controlled action. Shakespeare then shows how both these agencies,
separately or in uneasy combination, are finally incapable of resolving
the polarities that structure the play. I find a similar separation of
word and action—and the sequential embodiment of the disjointed
medium in fallible mediators of contrasting natures—in *Troilus and
Cressida* and, even more clearly, in *Measure for Measure.* In *Romeo*
and *Measure* the pattern is most clear at the moment when the action
switches abruptly from an inquiry into the arbitrational ability of
language to a similar interest in the efficacy of disciplined actions.
Juliet turns immediately to Friar Laurence as she dismisses her Nurse,
and the implied transition from the mode of language to the mode of
action underscores Shakespeare's sudden imposition of a dramatic
control upon a situation resistant to a linguistic solution. Duke
Vincentio, an obvious surrogate playwright, only seizes control of

Measure for Measure's action after language has totally broken down in the ethical morass that plagues Vienna: a breakdown illustrated most graphically perhaps in the wonderfully inane chatter of the bawd Pompey. In the contrasted figures of Pandarus and the wily dog-fox Ulysses (the main agents of *Troilus and Cressida*) we glimpse a similar dialectic, but the pattern becomes too complex for easy schematization once we progress to *King Lear* and *Timon of Athens*. Still, suiting the word to the action and vice versa continues to engage Shakespeare's attention.

The great discrepancies between the scatterbrained old Nurse and the ascetic Friar, the vulgar Pandarus and the philosophical Ulysses, the debauched Pompey and the altruistic Duke Vincentio reveal how drastically Shakespeare can at times polarize his medium into seemingly irreconcilable agencies representing the primacy of either the word or the act. Furthermore, I believe there is a valid critical perspective from which we can understand the dialectic created by those divergent figures: namely, Shakespeare's projection into the content and movement of the plays his own awareness of the divisive currents present in poetic drama. This perspective is difficult to sustain because it implies a self-conscious artist capable of concurrently launching his characters in action and critically observing his own play as it takes shape. But by granting Shakespeare that dual consciousness—the final extension of "negative capability"—it becomes possible to see how a great artist struggles to understand and master the full resources of his demanding medium. It is fairly clear, for instance, that characters like Friar Laurence, Duke Vincentio, and Edgar function at times as surrogate playwrights, thereby allowing Shakespeare to observe one aspect of his craft in operation. It may not be so readily perceivable that other quite different characters, like the Nurse, Pandarus, and even Pompey, body forth in a similar manner Shakespeare's awareness of the essentially linguistic capacities of his complex art. The drama resulting from the tension between the two competing forces of action and language is not only interesting in itself but also gives rise to a rich metadramatic commentary that suggests Shakespeare's feelings about what he has attempted to do and how well he has succeeded. My effort to follow Shakespeare through these difficult plays on this level of commentary is the most formidable, and hopefully rewarding, part of my task.

I TEMPERING EXTREMITIES

Hazardous Mediation in *Romeo and Juliet*

❧

Why the devil came you between us? I was hurt under your arm. (III.i.100–101)

❧

I

Modern commentary on *Romeo and Juliet* suffers from an apparent inability to move beyond a rather narrow range of received critical commonplaces. Since Harley Granville-Barker's influential "Preface" was first published in 1930, for instance, we rarely find a discussion of the play's construction that does not comment on the alleged "sense of swiftness" we supposedly experience as the play's action unfolds.[1] Granville-Barker spoke repeatedly of passages of dialogue "flashing by," of how "the action speeds on," and of how the audience is

[1] Harley Granville-Barker, *Prefaces to Shakespeare* (Princeton: Princeton Univ. Press, 1947), vol. 2, pp. 300–349. The phrases quoted are found on pp. 302, 307, and 311, but the idea of a rapidly expiring action is pervasive in the entire section entitled "The Conduct of the Action" (pp. 302–323). Madeleine Doran, *Endeavors of Art: A Study of Form in Elizabethan Drama* (Madison, Wis.: Univ. of Wisconsin Press, 1954), observes that "Shakespeare greatly intensifies the irony of the reversal by telescoping time and dovetailing events" (p. 297) in comparison to the older version of the story in a poem by Arthur Brooke, which was Shakespeare's source for the play. John Lawlor comments on "the onward drive of events" and of how "the nine months' action of Brooke's *Tragicall Historye* is crowded into a few days." See his essay *"Romeo and Juliet"* in *Early Shakespeare, Shakespeare Institute Studies,* ed. John Russell Brown and Bernard Harris (New York: Schocken Books, 1966), pp. 123–45. Mark Van Doren, *Shakespeare* (New York: Henry Holt, 1939), says "everything is sudden in this play. Its speed is as great as that of *Macbeth*" (p. 67). G. B. Harrison,

"sped on with little relaxation" from event to rapidly expiring event. Such an insistence on accelerated pace and continuous flow of action— Granville-Barker's general contribution to modern stage technique— should remind us that he was more successful as an innovative director of Shakespeare than as a critic of particular plays. Nevertheless, his point of view prospers, usually in combination with thematic investiga- tions that attempt to associate the formal emphasis on swiftness with the reiterated imagery of gunpowder and flashes of lightning, the great impetuosity of the young lovers, and the omens of imminent disaster that recur frequently throughout the play. Such general observations allow critics who adopt this approach to understand the play's structure as a formal mirroring of its theme: a theme approximated most suc- cinctly in Lysander's speech in *A Midsummer Night's Dream* that describes how "so quick bright things come to confusion" (*MND*. I. i. 149).[2] When we view it from this angle, the play appears formally neat and thematically simplistic; thus we can genially patronize it as the early work of a fine young dramatist, but one not yet fully responsive to the complexities of either the tragic experience or the medium of poetic drama. "The assured and studied neatness" of the play, as one recent critic puts it, "bespeaks a victory of art over materials rather too sub- missive to begin with."[3] Shakespeare emerges as a young dramatist who achieves mastery over his medium a bit too easily.

Shakespeare's Tragedies (London: Routledge and Kegan Paul, 1951), observes that the play "is a story of one hundred and twenty hours, set in the dog days of August when tempers are short and swords slip easily from their scabbards; and the whole effect is heightened by this increase in speed and movement" (pp. 48–49). Indeed, the concept of swift action is too commonplace to even summarize.

[2] Caroline F. E. Spurgeon, *Shakespeare's Imagery and What It Tells Us* (Cam- bridge: Cambridge Univ. Press, 1935, reprinted 1965), says the play is "building up a definite picture and atmosphere of brilliance swiftly quenched" (p. 316). Donald A. Stauffer, *Shakespeare's World of Images: The Development of His Moral Ideas* (New York: W. W. Norton, 1949), quotes the passage from *A Mid- summer Night's Dream* and claims that "Shakespeare finds the lightning-in-the- night adequate as the germinating and organizing symbol for *Romeo and Juliet*" (p. 54). In his "Introduction" to The Pelican Shakespeare edition of the play (Baltimore, Md.: Penguin Books, 1960), John E. Hankins also quotes the same passage and asserts that it "seems to contain the theme enlarged upon in *Romeo and Juliet*" (p. 16). Again this idea is too pervasive to make select documentation very helpful.

[3] James L. Calderwood, *Shakespearean Metadrama* (Minneapolis, Minn.: Univ. of Minnesota Press, 1971), p. 120. Although I disagree with this particular judg- ment, I have found Calderwood's general approach to *Romeo and Juliet* stimu- lating and helpful.

Such a general response to *Romeo and Juliet* is misleading because it blurs the distinction between theme and structure, allowing thematic considerations to serve speciously as formal investigations. Our actual encounter with the play's rising structure—its moving surface and linguistic texture—reveals a quite different picture of Shakespeare's involvement with his medium. Consider, for instance, Romeo's initial appearance near the end of the opening scene. A worried discussion between Montague and Benvolio concerning Romeo's recent anti-social behavior precedes his entrance. Romeo's father wishes he could "but learn from whence his sorrows grow" (I. i. 152), and Benvolio volunteers to question Romeo, promising the departing Montague to "know his grievance, or be much denied" (155). Upon Romeo's entrance, Benvolio begins forthrightly with the direct question, "What sadness lengthens Romeo's hours?" (161). Romeo's quibbling reply immediately deflects the conversation away from any simple exchange of information and launches it instead on a wayward course of rapidly increasing obfuscation.

> ROMEO. Not having that which having makes them short.
> BENVOLIO. In love?
> ROMEO. Out—
> BENVOLIO. Of love?
> ROMEO. Out of her favor where I am in love.
> (I. i. 162–66)

Given this unpromising beginning Benvolio cannot be too surprised when Romeo's responses further degenerate into an uninformative oxymoronic babble which threatens to continue until the powers of invention wane.

> O brawling love, O loving hate,
> O anything, of nothing first create!
> O heavy lightness, serious vanity, . . .
> (I. i. 174–76)

Yet, after twenty-two more lines of such discourse, Benvolio initiates another attempt to elicit a straight answer from his verbose friend: "Tell me in sadness [i.e., seriously], who is that you love?" (197). And while Romeo's response is not encouraging—"What, shall I groan and tell thee?"—Benvolio doggedly presses on and finally, after fifty lines of tedious verbal sparring, is rewarded with what appears in context to be a communicative breakthrough, although, in effect, farcically minimal and even redundant.

> ROMEO. In sadness, cousin, I do love a woman.
> BENVOLIO. I aimed so near when I supposed you loved.
> (I. i. 202–03)

Even this pitiful triumph in lucidity is clouded by Benvolio's unfortunate choice of words, for Romeo instantly seizes upon the "aiming" image as an occasion once more to detour the conversation into a wordy tangle of metaphoric amplification. When they finally clear this particular thicket of verbiage, Benvolio wisely does not pursue any further his futile quest. The two companions soon leave the stage with Benvolio, and the audience, still ignorant even of Rosaline's name. All we know is that Romeo is indeed sinking "under love's heavy burden," but we suspected that before his appearance. More importantly, we begin to sense that the ongoing impetus of the play is also burdening under the weight of retarding verbal excesses.

Only by contemplating the plot of *Romeo and Juliet* in the abstract does it become possible to speak reasonably of "the swift pace of the action."[4] To follow closely the concrete progression of the play is to become increasingly aware that the shaping impulse in the structure is frequently impeded by verbiage and clotted by rhetoric as it moves towards completion. Occasionally the language of the play creates a lucid and flexible medium for communication and dramatic continuity, but most often it tends towards a density and resistance, which causes the action to bog down into mindless chatter and self-serving verbosity. Perhaps nowhere is such verbosity more obvious than in the fifty-five lines of dialogue that open the play. The servants Sampson and Gregory move in an ambience of verbal anarchy where real communication is virtually impossible, since almost every word is subject to contradictory meanings, and where discourse seldom rises above the level of idiotic circularity.

> ABRAM. Do you bite your thumb at us, sir?
> SAMPSON. I do bite my thumb, sir.
> ABRAM. Do you bite your thumb at us, sir? . . .
> SAMPSON. No, sir, I do not bite my thumb at you, sir; but I
> bite my thumb, sir.
> GREGORY. Do you quarrel, sir?
> ABRAM. Quarrel, sir? No, sir.
> (I. i. 42–50)

4 The well-worn phrase is Douglas Cole's in his "Introduction" to *Twentieth Century Interpretations of "Romeo and Juliet"* (Englewood Cliffs, N.J.: Prentice-Hall, 1970), p. 10.

We need fear no violence from men so adept at evasive double-talk. It is only the untimely entrance of Benvolio, giving a sense of advantage to the Montague faction, that breaks the verbal deadlock and precipitates the fighting. Once violence does erupt, however, language gives way to mere noise and chaotic bustle, and sustained discourse can be re-established only with great effort. Witness Prince Escalus' frustration as he attempts to address his feuding subjects:

> Rebellious subjects, enemies to peace,
> Profaners of this neighbor-stainèd steel—
> Will they not hear? What, ho! you men, you beasts.
> (I. i. 79–81)

The sequence of events here suggests that action and language are just as polarized and hostile to each other as are the Capulets and Montagues. Synchronization of act and word appears impossible, which is clearly evident in Benvolio's futile attempt simultaneously to draw his sword and talk the servants into reconciliation. "What, drawn, and talk of peace?," Tybalt exclaims, "I hate the word / As I hate hell, all Montagues, and thee" (I. i. 67–68). But Tybalt's hatred of the word enjoys only a momentary ascendancy and quickly gives way to wordy recapitulations of past actions, first in Prince Escalus' summary of the feud and then in Benvolio's curiously unnecessary description of the fighting that just ended: only the first instance in a strange series of dramatically redundant recapitulations in the play.[5]

Inspection of the opening scene of *Romeo and Juliet* reveals how inadequate notions about the play's swift pace are. What we actually experience are rather static exfoliations of various forms of linguistic mismanagement (not just debased Petrarchanisms) punctuated by sudden explosions of destructive action. In this regard the opening scene prefigures a general dialectic in the play that opposes words and deeds, *verba* and *praxis,* in an irreconcilable hostility. More importantly, neither words nor deeds, in combination or separately, will be able to serve as an effective medium for viable human existence in the play. The two-fold inadequacy of mediation appears initially when Benvolio (his name means "good will") steps between the swords of the Capulets and Montagues and tries to use a blend of words and actions to arbitrate a reconciliation. The immediate consequence of his intervention is only an unexpected intensification of the violence. In fact, intermediaries in *Romeo and Juliet* repeatedly suffer shocking reversals when they try to

[5] See, for instance, III. i. 149–74; V. iii. 228–70; and V. iii. 272–90.

carry out their benevolent intentions. During a climactic episode in Act III Romeo will reenact Benvolio's futile gesture by boldly stepping between "the pass and fell incensèd points" of Mercutio's and Tybalt's rapiers (words and deeds in deadly conflict?) in a noble effort to arbitrate their differences. When Benvolio later recapitulates Romeo's intervention he stresses both its linguistic and physical aspects.

> Romeo he cries aloud,
> 'Hold, friends! friends, part!' and swifter than his tongue,
> His agile arm beats down their fatal points,
> And 'twixt them rushes.
> (III. i. 162–65)

Shakespeare's stage direction describes the immediate consequence of Romeo's attempt at mediation: "Tybalt under Romeo's arm thrusts Mercutio in" (88). Against the background of such recurring failures of mediation Mercutio's dying comment on Romeo's intercession transcends its immediate dramatic context and resonates through the whole play: "Why the devil came you between us? I was hurt under your arm" (III. i. 100–101). Mercutio's reference to the devil seems particularly fortuitous here, since both aspects of mediation, words and actions, will appear increasingly demonic before the play concludes.

The intense passion that draws Romeo and Juliet together, nourishes them in adversity, and finally unites them in death is unquestionably the source of the play's power over us. The preceding discussion establishes the peculiar context that sustains the young lovers as dramatic entities. Their gradual isolation from each other and from their intransigently hostile society occurs in a carefully delimited dramatic setting characterized by processes of flawed mediation, which terminate in acts of increasing violence. Thus, critical reassessments of the lovers' experience must respond to the play's focus on the related activities of various middlemen. Two characters are particularly important in regard to the lovers: the Nurse and Friar Laurence. It is the constant endeavor of those lively agents that makes *Romeo and Juliet* a dramatic action instead of something like a musical recitative. Without the intervention of the two figures both the lovers and the play would remain fixed in postures of extreme lyricism. They make the play move, albeit to an unintentional tragic conclusion, and it is their failures as successful mediators, more than anything else, that signal the inevitable suicides that resolve the action. Their dramatized inadequacies, however, are not so much character flaws as dual refractions of a medium antagonistic to purposeful human existence. The old Nurse, who toils for the lovers' delight by delivering love messages and acquiring ladders, embodies medium in the form of language. On the other hand, the Friar, who orders the despairing lovers to act according to prearranged plans, embodies medium in the form of action. The Nurse's silly chatter dominates the first half of the play and keeps the tone predominately comic, whereas Friar Laurence's somber control of the second half darkens the tone and gradually modulates the play into tragedy. Therefore, the opening scene's dramatization of a fundamental conflict between word and action extends, through the obvious incompatibility of the bawdy old lady and the austere friar, into the overall design of the play. The ludicrous juxtaposition of mediators may also be metadramatically significant, since Shakespeare's early development is marked by a concern with finding ways to reconcile both the poetic and dramatic imperatives of his craft.[6] It is possible to see Shakespeare "simultaneously scrutinizing characters in action and his own play in the making."[7] I will try to set forth these propositions more fully in the following sections.

II

The first half of *Romeo and Juliet* frequently brings people together for the purpose of exchanging information, but in most instances the encounters produce only a torrent of words, either in the form of wretched puns and choplogic or occasionally impressive rant and rhetoric, that result in general confusion or delayed and trivialized transfer of information. All the characters participate in this wordiness, but the Nurse and Mercutio set the basic tone. Their verbose digressions are delightful to us but exasperating to those in the play who have to suffer through them. For example, Mercutio's exhaustive amplification on Queen Mab impolitely interrupts Romeo's account of his omin-

[6] I am thinking in particular of S. T. Coleridge's remark that "in this tragedy the poet is not, as I have hinted, entirely blended with the dramatist." See *Shakespearean Criticism* ed. T. M. Raysor (London: Dent, Everyman Library edition, 1960), vol. 2, p. 102. Coleridge's point occasionally finds less subtle expression from modern critics, as in Norman Holland's blunt assertion that "Shakespeare's imagination in *Romeo and Juliet* is lyric, rather than dramatic," *The Shakespearean Imagination* (New York: Macmillan, 1964), p. 75. The issue, I hope to show, is much more complicated than this.

[7] I have borrowed this succinct phrase from T. McAlindon's "Language, Style, and Meaning in *Troilus and Cressida*," PMLA, 84 (1969), p. 43: a fine essay with some helpful insights into Shakespeare's struggle with the craft of play-making.

ous dream, delays their arrival at the Capulets' ball, and rambles on for forty-two excoriating lines before Romeo is finally able to silence him in mid-sentence with the rebuke, "Peace, peace, Mercutio, peace! / Thou talk'st of nothing" (I. iv. 95–96).[8] In the scene preceding that one the Nurse takes fifty-two lines of astonishing poetry to amplify her simple statement that Juliet is not yet quite fourteen years old. Only the combined pleas of Juliet and her mother succeed in finally plugging her repetitious flow of anecdotes, spontaneous reminiscences, and irrelevant observations. "Enough of this," Lady Capulet orders, "I pray thee hold thy peace" (I. iii. 49), but impetus alone carries her onward for another fourteen lines before she finally reluctantly stops. Shakespeare introduces both Mercutio and the Nurse in similar ways as essentially talkers of nothing whose flights of verbosity retard the action and clog the channels of communication. Romeo's concise description of Mercutio could apply equally well to the Nurse, to whom it is addressed: "A gentleman, nurse, that loves to hear himself talk and will speak more in a minute than he will stand to in a month" (II. iv. 139–41). Mercutio, of course, is quite conscious of the effect of his verbal gymnastics, whereas the Nurse is not. For instance, his dazzling description of Tybalt's fencing prowess—"Ah, the immortal passado! the punto reverso! the hay!"—draws from a bewildered Benvolio only a quizzical, "The what?" (II. iv. 25–27).

Benvolio is not the only character subjected to such linguistic overkill. Lady Capulet treats Juliet to an excessively amplified description of Paris as a "fair volume" (I. iii. 80–94); Capulet works through an elaborate conceit on the parallels between his weeping daughter and "a bark, a sea, a wind" (III.v.130–38); and even Juliet momentarily abandons herself in an oxymoronic lament on Romeo as "Beautiful tyrant! fiend angelical!" (III. ii. 73–85). Critics have often pointed out that such verbal excesses are meant to reveal inadequacies in the characters who succumb to them, which is probably true.[9] However, the

---

[8] We are reminded here of the similar relationship in *The Merchant of Venice* between Bassanio and Gratiano, Gratiano being a character who also "speaks an infinite deal of nothing" (I. i. 114).

[9] Norman Rabkin, *Shakespeare and the Common Understanding* (New York: The Free Press, 1967), offers a full demonstration of the subtle ways in which stylistic aberrations are associated with deficiencies in character. See pp. 162–84. See also Marion B. Smith, *Dualities in Shakespeare* (Toronto: Univ. of Toronto Press, 1966), pp. 100–09, who attempts a similar defense of the play's stylistic irregularities. Those arguments, and others like them, should be seen against the background of less enthusiastic commentary on *Romeo*'s style. Derek A. Traversi, *An Approach to Shakespeare* (Garden City, N.Y.: Doubleday, 1956),

general tendency of language to debilitate and obstruct action and human understanding in the play implies more than just a satiric intent. The wide scope of linguistic aberration suggests that Shakespeare is concerned with the more basic problem of the adequacy of language as a suitable medium for valid social communion. Nowhere do we feel that inadequacy more strongly than in the activities of the Nurse. She is both the most active mediator and the most irrepressible talker. "Send me word to-morrow," Juliet tells Romeo in the balcony scene, "By one that I'll procure to come to thee" (II. ii. 144–45). When Juliet's procuress approaches Romeo the next morning, Mercutio greets her with the words, "A bawd, a bawd, a bawd!" (II. iv. 122). The Nurse's secret activities as liaison for the lovers suggest that she is essentially a bawd.

> I must another way,
> To fetch a ladder, by which your love
> Must climb a bird's nest soon when it is dark.
> I am the drudge, and toil in your delight.
> (II. v. 72–75)

Like her medieval associate, Pandarus, the Nurse appears at times to function almost as a paradigm of external agency, of process and instrumentation.[10] Despite her age and bulk she is always on the go, hectically mediating between the static passivity of the lovers. "Hie to your chamber," she advises Juliet in Act III,

> I'll find Romeo
> To comfort you. I wot well where he is.
> Hark ye, your Romeo will be here at night.
> I'll to him; he is hid at Laurence' cell.
> (III. ii. 138–41)

It may seem that the lovers exacerbate their difficulties by acquiescing in the intervention of others, which is partly true. But the strong emphasis on the Nurse's role as go-between suggests that Romeo and Juliet

---

for example, says "Formal considerations . . . prevail over the full development of emotion, and the elaborate verbal pattern corresponds to considerations that are primarily literary and rhetorical, and only in a very secondary sense personal" (p. 18). Similar reservations are voiced by Granville-Barker, p. 301, and W. H. Clemen, *The Development of Shakespeare's Imagery* (London: Methuen, 1951), pp. 63–73.

[10] Philip Edwards, *Shakespeare and the Confines of Art* (London: Methuen, 1968), says of the Nurse, "She is the great good-hearted bawd of the play; it does not matter to her *whom* she brings to Juliet; either Romeo or Paris will do (p. 75).

can only activate their love through her agency. In this regard, among others, the lovers look forward to Troilus and Cressida and their dependency on Pandarus. Although the lovers may desire an immediate relation, they are doomed, Shakespeare seems to imply, by the inherent between-ness of human relationships to a contact based on mediacy.[11]

Shakespeare suggests the potentially tragic implications of a mediated relationship in scenes that reveal the grotesque inadequacy of the Nurse as a messenger of love. Her language constantly distorts, parodies, and vulgarizes the aspirations of the lovers.[12] When she meets Romeo in Act II on a mission of love, her natural stupidity and garrulity comically hinder any meaningful exchange of information. "Pray you, sir, a word," she says to Romeo, and launches into a verbal assault marshalled apparently to undermine all valid use of the word:

> and, as I told you, my young lady bid me inquire you out.
> What she bid me say, I will keep to myself; but first let
> me tell ye, if ye should lead her into a fool's paradise,
> as they say, it were a very gross kind of behavior, as
> they say. . . .
> (II. iv. 153–57)

She rambles on in this manner for some more lines until Romeo, growing anxious to discover Juliet's word of love through this smokescreen of verbal nonsense, manages to interject a half-completed comment. Alas, it only intensifies the growing confusion.

> ROMEO. Nurse, commend me to thy lady and mistress. I protest unto thee—
> NURSE. Good heart, and i' faith I will tell her as much. Lord, Lord! she will be a joyful woman.
> ROMEO. What wilt thou tell her, nurse? Thou dost not mark me.
> NURSE. I will tell her, sir, that you do protest, which, as I take it, is a gentlemanlike offer.
> (II. iv. 161–68)

[11] I am indebted to Sigurd Burckhardt for the distinction here between mediacy and immediacy and also for his many brilliant observations on Shakespeare's response to his medium. See his collected essays, *Shakespearean Meanings* (Princeton: Princeton Univ. Press, 1968). The essays entitled *"King Lear: The Quality of Nothing,"* pp. 237–59, and "The King's Language: Shakespeare's Drama as Social Discovery," pp. 260–84, are particularly helpful on the subject of medium.

[12] In this regard, too, she is a forerunner of Pandarus in *Troilus and Cressida*.

This exchange is good local comedy, of course, and looks forward to Mistress Quickly and Pompey Bum, but the fun also serves a serious purpose. Shakespeare makes us aware that the agent who must handle the lovers' communications is sadly lacking in the perquisite skills. Indeed, she is just as unlettered as the nameless messenger in Act I who tries unsuccessfully to deliver the invitations for the Capulets' ball. Shakespeare makes her illiteracy clear in the following exchange:

> NURSE. Doth not rosemary and Romeo begin both with a letter?
> ROMEO. Ay nurse; what of that? Both with an R.
> NURSE. Ah, mocker! that's the dog's name. R is for the—
> No; I know it begins with some other letter.
> (II. iv. 195–98)

The debilitating nature of the Nurse's language appears in her unintentional devaluation of Romeo's name to "the dog's name." Later on, she will tell Juliet that "Romeo's a dishclout" in comparison with Paris.

Romeo's communicative difficulties with the loquacious Nurse are fairly insignificant compared to those Juliet must endure. Juliet's relative immobility makes her particularly dependent upon the Nurse's transactions and, therefore, painfully vulnerable to her deficiencies. Act. II, scene 5, is entirely concerned with Juliet's frantic efforts to find out from the Nurse exactly what Romeo said concerning the marriage arrangements. Her first seventeen lines form a lament on her unhappy reliance upon an intermediary whom she accurately describes as "Unwieldy, slow, heavy and pale as lead" (II. v. 17). Juliet's desire is for an instantaneous, fully responsive medium for love's communications: "Love's heralds should be thoughts, / Which ten times faster glide than the sun's beams" (4–5). She feels that love's agent should be "as swift in motion as a ball" (13) so that "My words would bandy her to my sweet love, / And his to me" (14–15). The tennis metaphor underscores Juliet's wish that the words of lovers could be an active force moving easily to the beloved through a fully responsive and speedy medium. But the stormy entrance of the Nurse, after a long three hour absence, quickly dispenses with such fond hopes. Juliet greets her tardy messenger with an impatient "O honey nurse, what news?", but more than fifty exasperating lines of inane chatter ensue before the scatterbrained Nurse can find the means to deliver her quite simple message from Romeo. In between she regales Juliet with long-winded lamentations concerning her deteriorating physical condtion. Communication, too, is in a state of collapse.

> JULIET. What says he of our marriage? What of that?
> NURSE. Lord, how my head aches! What a head have I!
> It beats as it would fall in twenty pieces.
> My back a t' other side—ah, my back, my back!
> (II. v. 47–50)

At other tortuous moments her message almost comes into view only to suddenly evaporate at the last minute in some totally irrelevant after-thought.

> JULIET. Sweet, sweet, sweet nurse, tell me, what says my love?
> NURSE. Your love says, like an honest gentleman, and a courteous, and a kind, and a handsome, and, I warrant, a virtuous—Where is your mother?
> (II. v. 54–57)

In her hypnotic search for synonyms to prolong the process of expression, the Nurse simply loses sight of her original intention, and so the latter part of the sentence forgets the earlier part: a syntactical quirk endemic to her speech.

This scene is repeated in a more somber key in Act III, scene 2, when the Nurse returns from Verona's streets to inform Juliet of the disastrous consequences of the fight between Romeo and Tybalt. Once again Juliet precedes the Nurse's entrance with an impassioned speech in which she now voices her yearning for an elimination of all mediating agencies that keep her from Romeo. Juliet calls upon Phaëton to "bring in cloudy night immediately" so Romeo can "Leap to these arms untalked of and unseen" (III. ii. 4,7). Her desire now for a direct unmediated contact with her beloved leads her to assert that "Lovers can see to do their amorous rites / By their own beauties" (8–9). As if to comment ironically on Juliet's aspiration to abolish all between-ness, Shakespeare brings on not the expected bridegroom but the Nurse. He further emphasizes her tragic naivete by her greeting to the Nurse:

> O, here comes my nurse,
> And she brings news; and every tongue that speaks
> But Romeo's name speaks heavenly eloquence.
> (III. ii. 31–33)

The Nurse has indeed come to speak of Romeo, but the "heavenly eloquence" of her "tongue" is not apparent as she scatters ambiguous references to Tybalt and Romeo, death and banishment, and general lamentation for all concerned. Poor Juliet is driven to near distraction.

JULIET. Ay me! what news? Why dost thou wring thy
hands?
NURSE. Ah, weraday! he's dead, he's dead, he's dead!
We are undone, lady, we are undone!
Alack the day! he's gone, he's killed, he's dead!
(III. ii. 36–39)

Juliet and the Nurse talk at cross-purposes for over forty lines before
the Nurse answers "It did, it did!" to Juliet's question, "Did Romeo's
hand shed Tybalt's blood?" (72). But prolonged exposure to such
contagious linguistic disorder causes Juliet herself to become momentarily inflicted with the disease. Her fall into an oxymoronic tirade
on Romeo as a "Dove-feathered raven! wolvish-ravening lamb!" (76)
ironically recalls her comment earlier that "every tongue that speaks
/ But Romeo's name speaks heavenly eloquence" (32–33). She quickly
recovers her unqualified love for Romeo, but she has learned how
hostile and destructive language can be to the name of the beloved.
"What tongue shall smooth thy name," she asks herself, "When I,
thy three-hours wife, have mangled it?" (98–99). The scene concludes
with Juliet once again dispatching the Nurse to find Romeo and
bring him to her chamber. The Nurse is off on her last errand.

In the following scene Romeo, in despair over news of his
banishment, asks Friar Laurence, "How hast thou the heart, / . . . To
mangle me with that word 'banishèd'?" (III. iii. 48–51). The verbal
parallelism shows that both lovers experience at this turning point
in the play their inescapable bondage to a verbal medium that can
"mangle" their aspirations. The hope Juliet expressed in the balcony
scene that Romeo could "Retain that dear perfection which he owes /
Without that title" (II. ii. 46–47) has proved untenable. The lovers
must realize their love in the context of a debased language or seek
it in the silence of death. Thus, their linguistic style suggests a
gradual movement away from mere noise towards a silence beyond
speech and realizable only in death.[13] This progression is the reason
for the omnipresent activity of the Nurse as an intermediary for the
lovers in the first half of the play. She is undoubtedly one of Shakespeare's early triumphs in characterization, but her full contribution
to the play's meaning only emerges when we see her as part of a
larger configuration concerned with mediation. On the other hand,
we cannot fully grasp the tragic fate of Romeo and Juliet unless we
relate it to the comical arbitration of the Nurse.

[13] A fine discussion on this aspect of the play can be found in Calderwood,
pp. 105–08.

III

Friar Laurence does not take a very active part in the play's action until the second scene of Act III when Romeo flees to his cell after killing Tybalt. Until that moment he only appears in two short scenes, and the lively antics of the Nurse and Mercutio easily overshadow him. Because of his slow start critics often overlook his contribution to the play's meaning. Granville-Barker, in his discussion of the play's characters, dismisses him in a brief paragraph as only a "ghostly confessor" kept "shadowed in his cell" by Shakespeare.[14] One reason the ascetic Friar may appear somewhat alien to the world of *Romeo and Juliet* is that, despite an occasional tendency towards *sententiae* and didactic speculations, he reveals a clear antagonism towards the various forms of clever talk that pervade the play. Even more than the laconic Benvolio he believes that "The date is out of such prolixity" (I. iv. 3), and he seldom misses an opportunity to rebuke someone overly addicted to flights of verbosity. For example, Romeo's paradoxical description of his meeting with Juliet draws from the overtaxed Friar the blunt admonishment, "Be plain, good son, and homely in thy drift. / Riddling confession finds but riddling shrift" (II. iii. 55–56). Similarly, in Act IV he will quickly silence the long-winded lamentations of the Capulets, Paris, and the Nurse as they survey the supposedly dead Juliet with the terse command, "Peace, ho, for shame! Confusion's cure lives not / In these confusions" (IV. v. 65–66). At the end of the play he prefaces his summary of the lovers' final four days with the comment, "I will be brief, for my short date of breath / Is not so long as is a tedious tale" (V. iii. 229–30), and his summary is brief considering the many events he has to sum up.[15] Friar Laurence's distrust of mere talk suggests how radically different his intervention in the lovers' affair is to be from the Nurse's. When her words prove inadequate and destructive to their union, the lovers turn to the actions of the Friar.

Juliet's scornful renunciation of the Nurse's guidance at the end of Act III, scene 5 explicitly marks the transition that will fundamentally alter the second half of the play. Dismissing her as "Ancient damnation! O most wicked fiend!", Juliet concludes with the precise words:

[14] Granville-Barker, p. 330.
[15] It is certainly brief when compared to the long tale Arthur Brooke's Friar tells in the source. See Geoffrey Bullough, *Narrative and Dramatic Sources of Shakespeare* (New York: Columbia Univ. Press, 1957), vol. 1, pp. 358–62.

> Go, counsellor!
> Thou and my bosom henceforth shall be twain.
> I'll to the friar to know his remedy.
> (III. v. 241–43)

The last line recalls Romeo's exit line at the end of the balcony scene, "Hence will I to my ghostly father's cell, / His help to crave" (II. ii. 189–90), and reminds us that the Friar has been partially involved in the action for some time. He secretly marries the lovers, and after Romeo has killed Tybalt he insists that he overcome his despair. Thus, Shakespeare establishes his mediating role fairly early in the play, and Philip Edwards' remark that *"Romeo and Juliet* is clearly a play about two worlds, with the Friar in between, clumsily trying to unite them" is generally accurate, although the charge of clumsiness seems unfair.[16] The lovers accept the Friar's management of their affair because he exudes a natural confidence in man's ability to direct his life towards benevolent ends. Romeo accepts a chastening tongue-lashing from the Friar when he momentarily abandons manly control of himself and falls blubbering on the floor.

> Art thou a man? Thy form cries out thou art;
> Thy tears are womanish, thy wild acts denote
> The unreasonable fury of a beast.
> (III. iii. 109–11)

The same note is present in the Friar's rather tactless admonishment to Juliet to allow "no inconstant toy nor womanish fear / Abate thy valor" (IV. i. 119–20) as she faces the ordeal of the death-counterfeiting potion. It is important to note the Friar's optimistic sense of purposeful human action in order to gauge how completely his manly ideal collapses at the play's conclusion. As he approaches the tomb in Act V the Friar confesses that "Fear comes upon me. / O, much I fear some ill unthrifty thing" (V. iii. 135–36). Juliet kills herself, he later explains, after "a noise did scare me from the tomb" (262). And when the Watch discovers him, he appears to the Prince as "a friar that trembles, sighs, and weeps" (184).[17] Thus, the play gradually

---

[16] Edwards, p. 73. Although I disagree occasionally with Edwards' comments on the Friar, I have found his study of *Romeo and Juliet* one of the best recent attempts to account for the role of the Friar. See also the intelligent remarks of E. C. Pettet on the Friar's contribution, *Shakespeare and the Romance Tradition* (London: Staples Press, 1949), pp. 117–22.

[17] Harold C. Goddard has some useful comments on the collapse of the Friar into an image of fear, *The Meaning of Shakespeare* (Chicago: Univ. of Chicago

diminishes the proud Friar to the same impotent condition he had previously found so repugnant in Romeo.

Friar Laurence's management of the action does not come into full prominence until the first scene of Act IV, when Juliet appears at his cell and challenges him to the full exercise of his ability. The sudden decision of old Capulet to force her marriage to Paris has created a situation that seems beyond all arbitration to both Juliet and the Friar.

> JULIET. O, shut the door! and when thou hast done so,
> Come weep with me—past hope, past cure, past help!
> FRIAR. Ah, Juliet, I already know thy grief;
> It strains me past the compass of my wits.
> (IV. i. 44–47)

The Friar's last line echoes Romeo's earlier excuse to Mercutio for abandoning him after the Capulets' ball: "My business was great, and in such a case as mine a man may strain courtesy" (II. iv. 49–50). The parallelism reminds us how drastically the tone of the play has changed. It is clear that Juliet is determined to apply extreme pressure on the Friar's professed ability to regulate action. Like Romeo in the previous cell scene she draws a knife and threatens to use it on herself "If in thy wisdom thou canst give no help" (52). We may feel that the Friar is being unfairly forced to arbitrate a dilemma for which he cannot be held entirely responsible. In that regard he emerges as an interesting precursor of later tragic agents—such as Brutus, Hamlet, and Angelo—who are compelled to act in potentially destructive situations that are not of their own making. If he could foresee the dismal outcome of his forced intervention in the plight of the lovers he might reasonably exclaim, "O cursèd spite / That ever I was born to set it right!" (*Hamlet*. I. v. 188–89). Like Hamlet, moreover, he really has no choice but to intervene, as we see in the lucid exactness of Juliet's appeal.

> Therefore, out of thy long-experienced time,
> Give me some present counsel; or, behold,
> 'Twixt my extremes and me this bloody knife
> Shall play the umpire, arbitrating that
> Which the commission of thy years and art
> Could to no issue of true honor bring.
> (IV. i. 60–65)

Press, 1951), vol. I, pp. 137–38. "Fear," he says, "is the evil 'star' that crosses the lovers. And fear resides not in the skies but in the human heart" (p. 138).

Juliet sets forth the alternatives in precise terms. The arbitrator of the lovers' dilemma will be either the wise "counsel" of the Friar or the "bloody knife" she holds ready at her breast. The ominous fact that, for Juliet, the dagger is prematurely bloody seems to load the dice against the Friar. Shakespeare may also mean to remind us that earlier attempts at arbitration—Benvolio's intervention in Act I and Romeo's in Act III—have ended, not in reconciliation, but in swords and corpses. Friar Laurence launches his desperate plan in an atmosphere clouded with implications of failure.

Whereas the Nurse constantly loses her way in the mere processes of expression, the Friar always directs action towards an end product, or some clearly perceived goal. "In one respect I'll thy assistant be," he tells Romeo in Act II, perceiving that the successful alliance of the lovers "may so happy prove / To turn your households' rancor to pure love" (II. iii. 90–92). Under his guidance "pure love" will be realized not primarily through the medium of language but through the agency of wise goal-oriented action.[18] The Friar would project upon an uncertain future a carefully thought out plot designed to move the action towards a comic resolution: marriage and general restoration of social harmony. Indeed, Friar Laurence sounds almost like a dramatist mapping the rough outlines of a projected comedy as he sends Romeo back to Juliet.

> Go get thee to thy love, as was decreed,
> Ascend her chamber, hence and comfort her.
> But look thou stay not till the watch be set,
> For then thou canst not pass to Mantua,
> Where thou shalt live till we can find a time
> To blaze your marriage, reconcile your friends,
> Beg pardon of the Prince, and call thee back
> With twenty hundred thousand times more joy
> Than thou went'st forth in lamentation.
> (III. iii. 146–54)

The absurd exaggeration of "twenty hundred thousand times more joy" underscores the degree to which the Friar's eyes are naively fixed upon a happy end product and subtly suggests an imbalance as dangerous in its way as the Nurse's enslavement to process. The lovers become actors in the Friar's grandly conceived play. As he gives Juliet

---

[18] The kind of basic shift in structural procedure I am suggesting is implicit in the following comment by Nicholas Brooke: "The latter part of the play is rather burdened by the load of plotting which has to be expounded," *Shakespeare's Early Tragedies* (London: Methuen, 1968), p. 104.

final instructions on her difficult role he cautions her not to "abate thy valor in the acting it." And Juliet is aware of the challenge before her, remarking as she takes the Friar's potion, "My dismal scene I needs must act alone" (IV. iii. 19). For his play to succeed the Friar must exercise the same qualities that made Tybalt such a feared duellist: an ability to "keep time, distance, and proportion" (II. iv. 21). However, he masters those formal principles no more successfully than did Tybalt. The denouement of the Friar's drama is to occur in the tomb when Juliet awakens to the kind attentions of Romeo and the Friar. Unfortunately things go awry, particularly time and proportion. Romeo arrives too early, the Friar too late, and Juliet's awakening unhappily coincides with the unplanned arrival of the Watch. More importantly, proportion is violated because the crucial scene, in which Romeo is supposed to meet Friar John, never occurs. "As a man of affairs, poor Friar Laurence proved deplorable," Granville-Barker comments, "but he had imagination." [19]

The basis of the Friar's faith in the efficacy of human actions is his conviction that a middle ground of moderation exists, which, if conscientiously pursued, will allow for a human control of destiny.[20] He repeatedly expresses his sense of an operative *via media*. For instance, he cautions Romeo and Juliet before their wedding to "love moderately: long love doth so; / Too swift arrives as tardy as too slow" (II. vi. 14–15). "Uneven is the course; I like it not" (IV. i. 5), he says of Capulet's hasty plans for Juliet's marriage to Paris, and he feels compelled to "devise some mean" (V. iii. 240) to thwart that "immoderate" plan. Thus, he is the most likely person to arbitrate as the clashing extremes of the play close in. Shakespeare means him to represent the only course of action open to the distraught and harried lovers in the play's second half, and his eventual failure should suggest not so much a personal inadequacy as a general inadequacy in the play itself: a recognition that there is finally no viable middle ground in the polarized world of *Romeo and Juliet*. The rigorous logic of the play gradually cancels out alternative possibilities until only suicide is left as a valid mode of action open to the lovers. Romeo speaks truer than he realizes when he stands before Juliet's tomb and announces that "I come hither armed against myself" (V. iii. 65), for, in a manner prefiguring the last scenes of *Julius Caesar* and *Hamlet*, all the play's prominent charac-

---

[19] Granville-Barker, p. 303.

[20] This point is made in a rather different context by Joseph S. M. J. Chang in an excellent article entitled "The Language of Paradox in *Romeo and Juliet*," *Shakespeare Studies*, 3 (1967), 22–42.

ters finally stand armed against themselves. "All are punished" (V. iii. 295), Prince Escalus rightly concludes.

It is rather misleading, therefore, to comment as Edwards does on the Friar's "over-confidence in one's powers" and on his "considerable arrogance." "There is an awkward feeling," Edwards adds, "that the Friar is playing a dangerous game. He is playing about with death; he too is an ignorant and near-sighted man." [21] The Friar's precarious scheme does lead to the lovers' suicides, but the degree of truth in such literal observations cannot be amplified into a comforting theory of a tragic flaw that explains away Shakespeare's more disturbing insistence, which we perceive symbolically, that in a world like *Romeo and Juliet* all human plots, reasonable or emotional, are doomed to failure. By an inexorable process of elimination, the final arbitrator for Juliet becomes the "happy dagger" (i.e., felicitous, adequate) that she snatches from its sheath on Romeo's side and buries in her breast, just after the frightened and helpless Friar deserts her by rushing from the tomb. The scornful dismissal she directs at the last of her mediators—"Go, get thee hence, for I will not away" (V. iii. 160)—should recall her earlier farewell to the Nurse. Similarly, Romeo discovered just a few seconds earlier the only operative intermediary between himself and his extremes: "Come, bitter conduct," he says as he takes the deadly poison, "come, unsavory guide!" (166). Perhaps Shakespeare means us to hear in Romeo's invitation to death an echo of Juliet's earlier evocation of night, spoken as she impatiently awaited Romeo's arrival to consummate their marriage: "Come, gentle night; come, loving black-browed night; / Give me my Romeo" (III. ii. 20–21). The parallelism reminds us that the lovers, having exhausted all available forms of mediation, do finally achieve in death that direct immediacy they desired but could not sustain in their lives. Or should we say that Death, personified as the ultimate mediator, succeeds in uniting the lovers in "a dateless bargain" only after the dramatized failures of the Nurse and Friar? As they join Death, he joins them in an embrace of perpetual consummation that triumphs over the temporal realm they now willingly abandon.

IV

"Romeo, I come!" Juliet cries as she drinks the Friar's death-counterfeiting potion. Death, in the guise of potion and poison, becomes

[21] Edwards, p. 78.

the "unsavory guide" that delivers the lovers from an increasingly intolerable and alien existence; for in neither language nor action have they found a medium capable of uniting them to each other and to their society. One sign of the singular quality of their love is that they do not seem especially surprised or disillusioned by that gloomy discovery. Although he might reasonably have done so, Romeo, during his long speeches in the Capulets' tomb, voices no disapproval of the Friar's bungled efforts on their behalf. From the lovers' special angle of vision, in fact, the various mediating activities of both the Nurse and the Friar seem curiously irrelevant and run a course somewhat tangential to their deepest concerns. They do seek out and acquiesce in the agencies of Nurse and Friar, but in their expressions of total dedication there is rarely any strong suggestion that they conceive life itself to be an environment capable of accommodating the intensity of their passion. Juliet's attempt during the balcony scene to temper the extremity of Romeo's passion—telling him "This bud of love, by summer's ripening breath, / May prove a beauteous flow'r when next we meet" (II. ii. 121–22)—is a passing gesture towards temporality that she never repeats. Likewise, Romeo's hope that "all these woes shall serve / For sweet discourses in our times to come" (III. v. 52–53) is designed to cheer the despairing Juliet and carries very little real conviction. Instead, as their commitment to absolutism grows, they see their love as a radiant moment outlined against a background of negating blackness and death. Juliet's impassioned cry, "Give me my Romeo," moves rapidly over the brief span of the coordinating conjunction "and" from expectations of sexual fulfillment to seemingly incongruous thoughts of glorious death.[22]

> Give me my Romeo; and, when he shall die,
> Take him and cut him out in little stars,
> And he will make the face of heaven so fine
> That all the world will be in love with night
> And pay no worship to the garish sun.
> (III. ii. 21–25)

Likewise, on the occasion of his secret marriage to Juliet, Romeo can apparently express his intense joy only by placing it in the annihilating context of "love-devouring death."

> Do thou but close our hands with holy words,

---

[22] Brooke comments on the love-death equation in this passage and notes that "Juliet's speech is itself magnificently alive, but it leaps straight into death" (p. 101).

> Then love-devouring death do what he dare—
> It is enough I may but call her mine.
> (II. vi. 6–8)

Similarly, Juliet's tendency to speak of Death as her lover further delineates the peculiarly futureless quality of their love.

Such utterances also reveal that the love of Romeo and Juliet is just as polarized as the society that oppresses them. In their ecstatic juxtapositions of love and death the lovers seem willfully to eliminate all thought of any middle ground of accommodation and adjustment to life, thereby effectively voiding—before the unfolding dramatic action confirms it—any real possibility of successful mediation. The impulse to exclude the middle informs the occasions where the lovers attempt to bridge the chasm opening between their sense of exalted love and their awareness of an impinging reality that destroys it. In their most heightened expressions of love, for instance, a troublesome gap gradually opens between what they perceive as the reality of their situation and what they express emotionally as desire: "Ah, dear Juliet," Romeo says as he surveys her body in the tomb,

> Shall I believe
> That unsubstantial Death is amorous,
> And that the lean abhorrèd monster keeps
> Thee here in dark to be his paramour?
> (V. iii. 101–05)

And to Juliet's desperate attempt to prolong the marriage night, Romeo answers:

> I'll say yon grey is not the morning's eye,
> 'Tis but the pale reflex of Cynthia's brow.
> (III. v. 19–20)

The phrases "shall I believe" and "I'll say" reveal the subjective effort required of the lovers to lift those depressing moments from the level of fact to the level of imagination. "The emotional reality of love is triumphantly affirmed," C. L. Barber says of moments like these, but "we remain always aware of what in the expression is factual and what imaginary." [23] We must acknowledge the affirmation while also recognizing that no mediation could be expected to reconcile such mutually exclusive planes of experience. Hence, we can simultaneously see the

---

[23] C. L. Barber, *Shakespeare's Festive Comedy: A Study of Dramatic Form and its Relation to Social Custom* (Princeton: Princeton Univ. Press, 1959), p. 160.

failures of the Nurse and the Friar as both the cause of the lovers' deaths and the symbolic confirmation of a love hopelessly polarized from the outset.

There is another more formal sense in which the attempts to reconcile Romeo and Juliet to their Veronese community cannot hope to succeed: Shakespeare simply does not allow the lovers and their society to occupy mutually interdependent spheres of being. Such discrepancy is especially observable on the level of character presentation, where Juliet can reasonably pledge to "no longer be a Capulet" (II. ii. 36) and rightly say of Romeo that "Thou art thyself, though not a Montague" (II. ii. 39). Shakespeare has so sequestered his young lovers from any direct contact with or indebtedness to their debased society that they appear mostly free from all necessary social reciprocity. "Despite the importance of family," James Calderwood says of the lovers' apartness, "they are essentially unrelated, meeting as isolated individuals, rather than complex human beings with social, political, religious, and even national allegiances and responsibilities to contend with." [24] The play's ability to generate pathos stems largely from our sense that the innocent lovers are victimized by a society in whose corruption they do not participate. As freestanding entities they seem strangers in their own community. So we may feel a bit cheated when Shakespeare quickly resolves the play by neatly collapsing the lovers' story into the background of their brawling families: a sudden and willful violation of the mostly noncommunicative gap between the lovers and their society. The only unmediated space that does remain intact at the play's conclusion is that between the lovers themselves, who must face death alone without the satisfaction of sharing even a brief moment of recognition together.

The final reconciliation of the Capulet and Montague families does not carry much dramatic conviction, partly because of its brevity but also because so many members of the families have died (the two lovers, Paris, Tybalt, Mercutio, Lady Montague) or are in the process of dying (Lady Capulet, Friar Laurence). Prince Escalus' offer to "be general of your woes / And lead you even to death" (V. iii. 219–20) suggests that the entire play is now moving rapidly towards an imminent and inclusive death. Montague and Capulet may shake hands and talk of raising gold statues of the lovers, but our final sense is that the world of *Romeo and Juliet* is one of radical division and disjunction. As if to strengthen our conviction Shakespeare extends this disjunction

[24] Calderwood, p. 104.

beyond the confines of the play so as to inform the audience's mode of response to the tragic conclusion. The emotions generated by the final scene, that is, do not encourage a very strong emotional participation from the audience (as *King Lear,* for example, will do), but tend rather to turn inward on themselves and, thus, away from the audience.[25] Hence, the concluding couplet of Prince Escalus' stanzaic summary—"For never was a story of more woe / Than this of Juliet and her Romeo" (V. iii. 309–10)—is not only resoundingly terminal in its rhyme and rhythm but also formally completes the basic pattern of "death-marked love" outlined in the choral sonnet that opens the play. Such emphasis on formal closure wraps the play a bit too snugly within its delimited sphere and restricts its ability to reach out and trouble our contemplation of its overall beauty.

   We can see that the disjunctive vision and structure of *Romeo and Juliet* arises from the various forms of failed mediation recurring in the play. The inability of well-meaning mediators to "incorporate two in one" (this seminal phrase is spoken by Friar Laurence just before the secret wedding of Romeo and Juliet) informs and structures the play, giving it an added critical dimension which critics, who are sensitive to its organization by polarities, often overlook. We have seen that an area of intense mediation exists between the static extremes of Capulet and Montague, moonlit orchard and sun scorched marketplace, age and youth, life and death, and, of course, Romeo and Juliet. A significant portion of the play's dynamics is the result of the activities of various intermediaries, the most important of whom are the Nurse and the Friar. Friar John's excuse for failing to get through to Romeo in Mantua—they "Sealed up the doors, and would not let us forth" (V. ii. 11)—could serve as the play's final comment on the efficacy of those agencies, for they fail in all instances to resolve opposites. Moreover, by polarizing his artistic medium into the words of the Nurse and the actions of the Friar, Shakespeare finds a way to project into the play his own concern, at this early stage in his development as a poetic dramatist, with the seemingly conflicting claims of poetry and drama. *Romeo and Juliet* succeeds, of course, but we do not feel that Shakespeare has yet achieved that rich fusion of word and action that will soon become the mark of his creative genius. Thus, the first half of the play is mostly comic, excessively wordy, and dominated by the irrepressible but essentially directionless chatter of the Nurse, while the second half is more tragic, burdened

[25] Brooke observes that *Romeo and Juliet* "is a moving play, certainly, but it is also detached; it does not encourage a deep emotional involvement in the audience" (p. 81).

with fast moving action, and generally controlled by the Friar's plotting. (There is some blending and overlapping obviously, but the sense of disjunction remains dominant.) By distancing himself from the particular inadequacies of those surrogates, Shakespeare is able to clarify further his relation to his art. To see *Romeo and Juliet* in this manner is to acknowledge not only its own peculiar fascination but also its contribution to our general understanding of Shakespeare's deepening response to the complex challenge of his medium.

II MONUMENTAL MOCKERY

Troilus and Cressida and the
Perversities of Medium

But Pandarus—O gods, how do you plague me!
I cannot come to Cressid but by Pandar.
(I. i. 90–91)

The essential problem for the creative artist is to bring desired form out of his chosen medium: to achieve articulation and design in opposition to the undifferentiated contingency of his primary material. His conception of the creative enterprise, of the malleability of his medium, and of what constitutes successfully achieved form may, of course, vary greatly. Many artists struggle painfully with their unruly materials and eventually compromise, whereas others, more blessed, seem to conceive of their work as a relatively effortless and fully satisfying activity. Michelangelo's creative sovereignty over his medium results from his ability to conceive his figures as lying hidden in the blocks of marble on which he chooses to work, so that his task as a sculptor is merely one of removing the stone which covers them. His sense of omnipotence permits him to create artistic forms almost as optimistically and effortlessly as his God creates Adam in the Sistine Chapel fresco. Indeed, at such supreme moments Michelangelo seems to share with God a conception of medium as totally subservient and accommodating to the light touch of creation: a gracious blasphemy that catches perfectly the optimistic Renaissance aesthetic of *sprezzatura*.

Even Michelangelo, however, cannot sustain godlike supremacy over his material, and in several provocative works he appears to acknowledge that the invincibility of inert matter can almost neutralize even his creative powers. His statue of the Dying Slave, for instance,

29

suggests that moment when life capitulates before the relentless force of dead matter. A more extreme instance of artistic impotence is present in his haunting statue of Saint Matthew. Michelangelo represents the saint as struggling in tortuous agony as if he were trying desperately to free himself from the imprisoning block of marble that contains him. In other words, the artist seems aware here that his medium is itself capable of successfully resisting his efforts to master it with fully achieved form. There is perhaps even a suggestion of something demonic and negating in the medium's ability to distort, frustrate, and debilitate the artist's effort at creation: a suggestion of encroaching chaos. At any rate, Michelangelo as creator has made himself very much a part of the statue's total statement, a statement that seriously qualifies the creative optimism informing his other works.[1]

Of course, a radical difference exists between the medium available to the sculptor and painter and the medium available to the dramatist. Yet the dramatist's response to the basic need to confront and master his materials may reveal attitudes towards creation similar to those already mentioned. Like Michelangelo, Shakespeare often conceives of artistic creation as an optimistic and relatively effortless activity. There is, perhaps, a basic truth behind the venerable assertion of Heminge and Condell in the *Folio* that "his mind and hand went together: and what he thought, he uttered with that easiness, that we have scarce received from him a blot in his papers." Notably similar to the claim of the conjunction of Shakespeare's mind and hand is Theseus' expression, in his famous comment on imagination in *A Midsummer*

---

[1] In the chapter entitled "The Poet as Fool and Priest: A Discourse on Method," Sigurd Burckhardt examines the artist's confrontation with his medium and asserts that "it is evident that the sculptor—or painter, or musician—cannot negate; he cannot express 'There is no War,' since War, even to be negated, must be physically there" *Shakespearean Meanings* (Princeton: Princeton Univ. Press, 1968), p. 34. Burckhardt extends the issue to the poet, claiming that "negation poses for the poet a crucial problem: it denies the existence of something which, simply by mentioning, it affirms, almost creates" (pp. 33–34). It is perhaps true that anything which fully emerges from the artist's prime material necessarily has a positive, undeniable existence. But Burckhardt has nothing to say here about the negating force of such strangely unfinished works of art as Michelangelo's Saint Matthew, which seem unable to achieve full articulation. However, my quibble on this point should be understood as further testimony of my general indebtedness to Burckhardt's several stimulating essays on Shakespeare's ongoing exploration of his medium. I have been aided in my understanding of Michelangelo's changing relationship to his medium by E. H. Gombrich, *The Story of Art* (London: Phaidon Paperback, 1950), pp. 220–29. See, in particular, his remarks on the Dying Slave, p. 227.

Night's Dream, of the perfect ease and power with which the poet captures the ideas his imagination creates. His sovereignty transforms an insubstantial idea into a concrete image with a gesture of dominance that suggests an almost totally unresisting and accommodating medium.

> And as imagination bodies forth
> The forms of things unknown, the poet's pen
> Turns them to shapes, and gives to airy nothing
> A local habitation and a name.
> (V. i. 14–17)

The syntactical parallelism of the statement "And as . . . , / the poet's pen" supports the claim for an effortless translation of image into fully realized form. Moreover, this clausal balance encourages us to see the two actions of perception and realization as occurring simultaneously, so that the poet's medium appears completely nonresistant and even non-temporal. If we scan the passage metadramatically—as we seem encouraged to do—we observe that Shakespeare allows the play's authority figure to describe a poet who brings form and shape out of nothing with the same omnipotence and graceful immediacy with which Michelangelo—and Michelangelo's God—brings life and form to Adam, and this poet may seem to us to bear a striking resemblance to the Shakespeare who wrote the play. Indeed, in plays like *A Midsummer Night's Dream*, *I Henry IV*, and *As You Like It* Shakespeare achieves such an astonishing poise and balance—both in content and form—of widely discrepant materials that we may reasonably feel that the godlike creation of Theseus' poet has actually been realized.

Although Theseus' aesthetic of rational order and control may appear to be in the ascendant in several plays of this period, it would be a serious error to regard that benign aspect as more than simply one phase in Shakespeare's constantly changing exploration into the potentialities of his medium and his ability to master it with meaningful forms.[2] Even in those three perfectly crafted plays, in fact, it is

---

[2] The metadramatic dimension of Shakespeare's art—his consciousness of the theatrical context of his craft—has been attracting increasing critical attention recently. Aside from the aforementioned work of Burckhardt, I have found the following books especially helpful: Anne Righter, *Shakespeare and the Idea of the Play* (London: Chatto & Windus, 1962); Nicholas Brooke, *Shakespeare's Early Tragedies* (London: Methuen, 1968); Philip Edwards, *Shakespeare and the Confines of Art* (London: Methuen, 1968); Eugene Paul Nasser, *The Rape of Cinderella* (Bloomington, Ind.: Indiana Univ. Press, 1970). This approach has been formulated most clearly, and applied quite intelligently, by James L. Calderwood in *Shakespearean Metadrama* (Minneapolis, Minn.: The Univ. of

possible to detect some growing discomfort on Shakespeare's part: a disturbing feeling that dramatic form and linguistic facility are triumphing rather too easily over the problems raised in the play-world. Furthermore, Shakespeare's apparent need to sustain a tacit commentary on his creative development is one reason for the complex fascination the plays have for us. The confrontation between artist and medium assumes a bleaker and more pressing character as Shakespeare matures as a playwright. *Troilus and Cressida* becomes less of an aberration and more of an instance of great significance for Shakespeare's development when we see it against this darkening background, for perhaps no other play raises the issue of the artist's struggle to master his materials quite so intensely as *Troilus* does.[3] This deeply troubling play seems to be the work of a dramatist no longer in serene control of his craft and, indeed, perilously close to capitulating before a medium that appears to have grown hostile and intransigent to his creative efforts.

To grasp more clearly the nature of the radical change in Shakespeare's attitude towards artistic creation, let us place beside Theseus' lines about the poet the following lines spoken by another legendary leader, Agamemnon. Meditating early in the play on the frustrated course of his seige of Troy, he counsels patience and fortitude:

> Sith every action that hath gone before,
> Whereof we have record, trial did draw
> Bias and thwart, not answering the aim
> And that unbodied figure of the thought
> That gave't surmisèd shape.
> (I. iii. 13–17)

Although explicitly about the need for stoic endurance in warfare, Agamemnon's words suggest a poetic quite different from that ex-

---

Minnesota Press, 1971). However, neither Calderwood nor any of the others, Edwards excepted, considers *Troilus and Cressida* from the metadramatic point of view.

[3] Philip Edwards has a fine discussion of *Troilus* along these lines. He speaks suggestively of the play as "somehow 'anti-art' or 'pre-art' in its refusal of a coherent form which might work against the picture of incoherence which is the matter of the play. . . . it refuses all resolution and consolation" (p. 107). Edwards' analysis builds upon a method for dealing with *Troilus'* formal and thematic peculiarities first set forth by Una Ellis-Fermor in her well-known essay, "'Discord in the Spheres': The Universe of *Troilus and Cressida.*" The essay appears in her book, *The Frontiers of Drama* (London: Methuen, 1946) pp. 56–76. "The materials of *Troilus and Cressida*," she asserts, "are more obviously at war than those of any other play of Shakespeare's" (p. 59).

pressed by Theseus. The accentuated inclusiveness of the royal sentiment ("every action that hath gone before, / Whereof we have record")
implies that all creators—whether warriors or dramatists—must not
expect mastery over their media or even effective control of the final
consequences of their activities. Here every idea that is realized in action
is only done so after great strain, and the final result is often less than
the initial conception.

Agamemnon's gloomy and fatalistic ethic becomes sympto-
matic of the prevailing attitude in the play, since most of the other
characters also voice similar skeptical sentiments concerning the possibility of ever achieving their desired goals. The heroic characters constantly complain of a lack of relation between intention and event, and
the unanimity of their expressions of expected frustration seems finally
to override considerations of character and to suggest qualities and attitudes pertinent not only to the world of the play but to the actual
form of the play itself. "One occasionally has the strong impression,"
as T. McAlindon succinctly observes, "that Shakespeare is simultaneously scrutinizing characters in action and his own play in the
making."[4] As often happens in Shakespeare's plays, we see technique
itself becoming the vehicle of theme as Shakespeare ostensibly locates
his own activity of artistic shaping within the perceiver's field of vision
and response. If *Troilus* fails "to satisfy as a work of art usually satis-
fies,"[5] it may be because the play is about the failure to create a meaningful order out of seemingly intractable materials: a failure that
encompasses both the substance and structure of the play. And if this is
so, we should discern a wider application than is generally realized in
Agamemnon's conviction that hope for "all designs begun on earth
below / Fails in the promised largeness" (I. iii. 4–5). Implicit in the
General's remark may lie a metadramatic critique not only of the play
itself but of playmaking in general.

I

We may more clearly see the aesthetic dilemma Shakespeare
confronts in *Troilus* if we understand the nature of the pessimism

---

[4] T. McAlindon, "Language, Style, and Meaning in *Troilus and Cressida*," PMLA,
84 (1969), p. 43. This essay offers a useful analysis of disjunct style and dissonant
language in *Troilus,* relating these defects to Shakespeare's "consciousness of the
requirements and pitfalls of his art" (p. 42). Like Edwards and Ellis-Fermor,
he concludes that "*Troilus and Cressida* is the work of an acutely self-conscious
artist" (p. 43).

[5] Edwards, p. 107.

voiced by the characters and the kinds of difficulties they face. As Ulysses addresses Nestor concerning his plot to reactivate Achilles by praising Ajax, he instinctively frames his words so as to color his scheme beforehand with the ambient sense of expected obstruction and frustration. "I have a young conception in my brain; / Be you my time to bring it to some shape" (I. iii. 312–13). Ulysses is a relatively active and generally hopeful character, yet even here the gloomy note of resignation is present in the mutely sounded but unpromising phrase, "bring it to some shape." After lengthily discussing the plot with Nestor, Ulysses finally sums up in terminology that even more clearly emphasizes the underlying sense of meaningless drift and almost certain failure regarding the proposed strategy. "But, hit or miss, / Our project's life this shape of sense assumes" (I. iii. 383–84). With Ulysses' project, which takes up a large part of *Troilus,* initiated in that skeptical manner, we are not really surprised to learn from Thersites in Act V that "the policy of those crafty swearing rascals . . . is not proved worth a blackberry" (V. iv. 9–11).

Ulysses is not the only character who appears to be engaged in a hopeless struggle with his own intimations of futility. We noticed above how Agamemnon and Nestor ineptly guide the Grecian army knowing that "The ample proposition that hope makes / In all designs begun on earth below / Fails in the promised largeness" (I.iii.3–5). Cressida espies "more dregs than water" (III. ii. 63) in the fountain of her love for Troilus yet fatally embraces it anyway. Troilus, too, knows at some level of his being that Cressida cannot be true to him, for her fidelity, even at the height of his infatuation, has only a hypothetical reality.

> O! that I thought it could be in a woman—
> As, if it can, I will presume in you—
> To feed for aye her lamp and flames of love;
>
> .   .   .   .
>
> How were I then uplifted!
> (III. ii. 150–60)

In his capacity as warrior Troilus is equally untroubled when Cassandra prophesies the total annihilation of Troy, since, as he explains to Hector, "We may not think the justness of each act / Such and no other than event doth form it" (II. ii. 119–20). Hector also seems only half aware that Achilles speaks prophetic truth when he predicts in precise detail how he soon intends to kill him, and he responds defiantly, "Wert thou an oracle to tell me so, / I'd not believe thee" (IV. v. 251–52). Cassandra's centrality in the pattern of prophesy should remind us that all the characters move in an atmosphere dense with implications of imminent catastrophe: an atmosphere that tends to throw the launching of human actions into an ironic and baleful light.

What is particularly noteworthy in those expressions of skepticism is the recurrence of language related to structure: surmised shape, all designs, shape, shape of sense, form, and many other words of a similar nature. For instance, on the night before Hector's death Andromache dreams of nothing "but shapes and forms of slaughter" (V. iii. 12) and Agamemnon greets Hector after the Act IV duel with these gloomy words: "Understand more clear, / What's past and what's to come is strewed with husks / And formless ruin of oblivion" (IV.v.164–66). As a consequence of such a continuous undertone of skepticism, a deep irony informs all talk of "designs" undertaken in *Troilus*. As Hector makes his sudden capitulation in the Trojan council scene, for instance, Troilus joyfully exclaims, "Why, there you touched the life of our design" (II. ii. 194). We know, however, that there is even less life in Troilus' design than in Ulysses' project, for Cassandra's prophetic words are still ringing in our ears: "Cry, Troyans, cry! . . . / Troy must not be, nor goodly Ilion stand" (II. ii. 108–09). When we survey these diverse sentiments it becomes clear that there is an operative disjunction in *Troilus* between the surmised shapes of the imagination and the actual realization of those shapes.[6] It is in that inclusive sense that Troilus' oft-quoted statement to Cressida about the "monstruosity in love" transcends its immediate dramatic context and resonates through the whole fabric of the play: "that the will is infinite and the execution confined; that the desire is boundless and the act a slave to limit" (III. ii. 75–77).

At this point we might well complain, as Agamemnon does after Ulysses' diagnosis of the war's stalemate, "The nature of the sickness found, . . . / What is the remedy?" (I. iii. 140–41). If there is a radical flaw in the nature of action itself, which obstructs and

[6] Such an operative disjunction is not more peculiar to *Troilus* than to other plays, however. Shakespeare's tendency to exploit the disjunction between human desires and the ability to realize those aspirations through purely human agency is a fundamental element in virtually every one of his plays. Moreover, this disjunction need not necessarily lead to catastrophe and a sense of despair, as it does in *Troilus*. It can serve a benign function and lead to wonder and a sense of mysterious fulfillment, as in some comedies and the late romances. What is perhaps unique about *Troilus* in this regard is its purely secular setting: its absolute absence of any sense of grace or other hints of supra-human intervention or guidance to save man from his own ineptitude.

debilitates the desired ends of action, as the characters continually imply, then what exactly is the nature of that intractable force and how does it manifest itself in the dramatic action of the play?

Perhaps it will be profitable briefly to recall how Michelangelo was able to achieve such striking effect in his statue of Saint Matthew by representing the figure of the saint in an unsuccessful struggle to liberate himself from the recalcitrant marble block. In that manner Michelangelo was able to throw significant emphasis, both thematically and formally, on the medium itself. We can also trace the omnipresent sense of frustration and stalemate in *Troilus* to a consciousness in the play of the intransigence of medium. Medium in this irreducible sense transcends the recognizable differences between sculptor and dramatist in that it stands for whatever seems to reside between impulse and achievement: whatever power, emotional or elemental, intervenes between desire and fulfillment. Thus understood, medium should suggest primary concepts of transmission such as agency and instrumentality. In other words, medium is whatever a creator perceives to exist between his apprehension of a whole harmonious design and his ability successfully to execute it.[7] In *Troilus,* as in *Romeo and Juliet,* these concepts do not rest on the level of abstraction but rather tend towards a dramatic concreteness of significant impact, a materiality that makes it possible for them to function in the play's ongoing action as active antagonists: "Checks and disasters / Grow[ing] in the veins of actions highest reared" (I. iii. 5–6).

By examining the dynamics of *Troilus'* plot, it becomes immediately apparent that an inordinate amount of the actual business of the play is given over to the mediating and conveying of persons, objects, or information from one party to another. It also becomes clear that crucial metaphysical and ontological questions of value and identity hinge on the nature and outcome of these various transactions.[8] The

[7] Burckhardt's provocative discussions of the challenging nature of the poetic dramatist's medium lie behind my understanding of the obstructing capability of medium in general, and I have profited greatly from these investigations. However, I feel that Burckhardt's focus is unnecessarily limited to the dramatist's struggle with language.

[8] The play's obsession with processes of mediation, the relation of identity to the definitions of others, and the philosophical issues of value and purposive human action, are central concerns of Terence Eagleton in his study of the play in *Shakespeare and Society: Critical Studies in Shakespearean Drama* (New York: Schocken Books, 1967), pp. 13–38. Eagleton notices the predominance of mediating activities and says "that describing someone to someone else is more than

Greeks intend to fight the Trojans until they deliver Helen, and in the council scene the Trojans debate at length the significance of her possible return. They recall the shadowy figure of Hesione, Ajax's mother and Priam's sister, whom "the Greeks held captive" (II. ii. 77). The Trojan seer Calchas defects to the Greeks and in exchange for safety incurs "a traitor's name" (III. iii. 6). Finally, as a result of Calchas' intercession, the Greeks return the captive Antenor to Troy in exchange for the seer's daughter Cressida, whom Diomedes conveys to the Greeks, and the play gives lavish attention to all the details of that exchange. Aeneas suddenly appears as a herald in the middle of the Greek war council to deliver Hector's challenge to duel with a Greek champion "midway between" the Greek tents and the walls of Troy. When the play opens Thersites belongs to Ajax, but we learn in Act II that "Achilles hath inveigled his fool from him" (II. iii. 87). Thersites bears letters from Achilles to Ajax and presumably from Hecuba and Polyxena to Achilles. Agamemnon's grand sentiments often find themselves rechanneled to his officers through the verbose and slightly comical expression of Nestor: "Nestor shall apply / Thy latest words" (I. iii. 32–33). Aeneas translates Troilus' identity to Ulysses who in turn passes it on to Agamemnon (IV. v. 95–112). Ulysses has "derision med'cinable / To use between" the pretended "strangeness" of the Greek leaders and Achilles' pride (III. iii. 44–45). Pandarus mediates our first view of the Trojan warriors with a running commentary (I. ii. 168–242), and Alexander explains Ajax's strange identity ("half Troyan, and half Greek") to Cressida (I. ii. 12–29). Pandarus conveys Troilus' "words, vows, gifts, tears, and love's full sacrifice" (I. ii. 268) to Cressida, and he also relays Cressida's beauty and reticence back to Troilus. Between the stalemated armies, between the static passivity of the lovers, exists an area of rather hectic mediations. In that regard *Troilus* is significantly like *Romeo and Juliet,* where much of the action centers on the mediating activities of the Nurse and Friar Laurence. As in the earlier play, what is particularly noteworthy in all these exchanges is that the desired transaction is most often marred or frustrated by the unpredictable processes of mediation.

The name Pandarus suggests the degree to which *Troilus* has incarnated dramatically the concept of the mediator as go-between.

---

a second-hand process, it is a way of actually mediating and conveying their reality to another, recreating them as individuals" (p. 14). Eagleton's study has helped me better to understand mediation in *Troilus* and in Shakespeare in general.

The image of the middleman informs Ulysses' plot to make Ajax Hector's opponent in the duel, and it lies at the base of the whole framing story of Paris' rape of Helen. Nowhere is it more clearly operative than in the words and actions of Pandarus.[9] He functions in the play's action to body forth the problems that medium presents both to the characters and to Shakespeare. His part should perhaps be understood as an intensification of the role played by the Nurse in *Romeo and Juliet*. As Harry Berger, Jr., observes, Shakespeare does not even bother to give psychological motivation to Pandarus' behavior. "He appears simply as a go-between. . . . He is the paradigm of pure external agency: a communicator of the parts of others, with no privacy or privation of his own."[10] Pandarus describes himself as a "broker," a "trader," a "go-between," a "broker-between," an "agent," and he is referred to by others as a "bawd," a "convoy," and a "broker-lackey." To Troilus he is Charon in his ferry at one instant and Cupid with his wings the next (III. ii. 9–14), but despite all fanciful euphemisms and metaphors we never forget that he is essentially a conveyance, an active mediator. Moreover, he himself knows the nature of his role in the play and never attempts to disguise it. "I have had my labor for my travail," he tells Troilus petulantly at the beginning of the play, "gone between and between, but small thanks for my labor" (I. i. 67–69). Halfway through the play he tells the lovers that "if ever you prove false one to another, since I have taken such pains to bring you together, let all pitiful goers-between be called to the world's end after my name" (III. ii. 190–93). He begins his last speech with the lament, "O world, world! thus is the poor agent despised" (V. x. 35–36). Indeed, at the play's unusual conclusion he actually serves as intermediary between the play-world and the contemporary audience, thereby extending the issue of mediation from the internal workings of the play to the actual theatrical experience. Like the "prologue armed" who introduces the play, Pandarus in the epilogue presents himself as "suited / In like conditions as our argument" (Pro., 24–25). For in an inclusive and radical sense Pandarus personifies the central themes in *Troilus* of between-ness, agency, process, and mediation. When we experience his role in this manner we realize that the most revealing and despair-

[9] Eagleton says, "The image of the merchant, the mediator, the go-between dominates the play, most obviously in Pandarus, but also in the plotting of Ulysses to set Ajax on to duel with Hector" (p. 15).
[10] Harry Berger, Jr., *"Troilus and Cressida*: The Observer as Basilisk," *Comparative Drama*, 2 (1968–69), p. 33. Berger's few remarks on Pandarus' agency nicely complement those of Eagleton.

ing words in the play are Troilus' plaintive "O gods, how do you plague me! / I cannot come to Cressid but by Pandar" (I. i. 90–91).

II

How are we then to understand Troilus' cry that he "cannot come to Cressid but by Pandar"? Is Troilus passively indulging an irresponsible penchant for delegating action to inferiors who can conveniently bear the blame for possible failure? or does that "cannot" signify the imposition of an inescapable limitation on the freedom of choice and action granted Troilus within the play? The strong emphasis on mediation traced above would seem to suggest the latter: that is, if Troilus is to activate his love for Cressida at all it can only be through the agency of Pandarus. The situation of Troilus and Cressida, therefore, is not too different from the necessarily mediated situation of Romeo and Juliet. By constructing the play in this manner Shakespeare again calls attention to the inherent between-ness of all human relationships: to the potentially tragic fact that all communication between selves is an exchange based on mediacy, not immediacy.[11] Shakespeare presents Troilus, Pandarus, and Cressida as they traditionally were in his medieval sources: three inextricably bound components of a fascinating and tragic configuration representing love in action. Shakespeare underscores the indissoluble nature of the trio at the climax of the assignation scene, when the three principals take hands to form an eternal contract. "Go to, a bargain made; seal it, seal it," Pandarus chants. "I'll be the witness. Here I hold your hand, here my cousin's" (III. ii. 189–90). What literary tradition and Shakespeare have so joined, let no Bradleian criticism put asunder.

The contractual language Pandarus continually uses in this scene directs us to the particularly modern touch Shakespeare brings to the venerable configuration. As agent, broker, and trader, Pandarus provides dramatic focus for a metaphoric web of references that use, as an organizing principle, imagery and diction associated with merchandising. As William R. Elton has shown, *Troilus* is loaded with "terms and concepts . . . relating to exchange, commerce, estimation, worth, price, buying and selling, trading, and so on."[12] This

[11] I have taken the distinction between mediacy and immediacy from Burckhardt's essay *"King Lear*: The Quality of Nothing," in *Shakespearean Meanings,* pp. 237–59.
[12] William R. Elton, "Shakespeare's Ulysses and the Problem of Value," *Shakespeare Studies,* 2 (1966), p. 95.

language is particularly significant since it helps reinforce the mediated nature of human relationships in the play. For instance, as Troilus glosses his predicament, he too uses commercial terminology to erect a metaphoric framework that will structure the various interactions of character in the rest of the play.

> Tell me, Apollo, for thy Daphne's love,
> What Cressid is, what Pandar, and what we.
> Her bed is India; there she lies, a pearl.
> Between our Ilium and where she resides
> Let it be called the wild and wand'ring flood,
> Ourself the merchant, and this sailing Pandar
> Our doubtful hope, our convoy and our bark.
> (I. i. 94–100)

These lines are crucial for a proper understanding of the dynamics of character interaction in *Troilus*. Inspired perhaps by Apollo, Troilus imagines himself as a merchant and Cressida as the desired merchandise, the pearl; he conceives of Pandarus as the all-important middleman, his agent in this transaction. That Troilus assigns to himself and Cressida purely static roles seems a severe liability. Troilus clearly is no Bassanio, no Romeo who can say of Juliet: "Wert thou as far / As that vast shore washed with the farthest sea, / I should adventure for such merchandise" (II. ii. 82–84). Only Pandarus has freedom of movement, and this mobility combines with what Edwards terms an "unromantic earthiness" and "commonness of valuation" to make him perhaps the most realistic member of the triad.[13] Here again, he may remind us of Juliet's Nurse with her combination of bustle and creaturality. Moreover, the whole success of Troilus' trading enterprise seems unfairly placed on his shoulders. Emphasis falls heavily on the risks involved in the endeavor: it is "a wild and wand'ring flood" upon which Pandarus must metaphorically sail. Troilus' skepticism concerning the outcome of the venture appears in his uncertainty over Pandarus' seamanship: "this sailing Pandar / Our doubtful hope, our convoy and our bark."

      To take a moralistic line of argumentation at this point and criticize Troilus, and Cressida too, for exacerbating their impotence by fatuously relying on Pandarus to bring them together may be an appealing alternative for some critical sensibilities. However, if Pandarus epitomizes medium in the irreducible sense outlined above, it

---

[13] Edwards, pp. 97, 101.

is difficult to see what other options are open to the lovers in the play. Shakespeare's real interest, it seems, is less in analysis of character than in a tragically conceived pattern of desire, endeavor, and achievement in which individual choices affect the outcome only indirectly.

The commercial scheme Troilus describes above is not peculiar to his existential situation. He reminds his fellows in the Trojan council scene that Paris, another agent of equally doubtful sailing credentials, was dispatched on a similarly precarious voyage for exactly the same kind of merchandise. He uses the same three-part metaphoric pattern with only the names changed. The Trojan Princes replace Troilus as the merchant; Paris replaces Pandarus as the venturesome agent; and Helen replaces Cressida as the pearl.

> It was thought meet
> Paris should do some vengeance on the Greeks.
> Your breath with full consent bellied his sails;
> The seas and winds, old wranglers, took a truce
> And did him service; he touched the ports desired,
> And for an old aunt whom the Greeks held captive
> He brought a Grecian queen, whose youth and freshness
> Wrinkles Apollo's and makes stale the morning.
> Why keep we her? The Grecians keep our aunt.
> Is she worth keeping? Why, she is a pearl
> Whose price hath launched above a thousand ships
> And turned crowned kings to merchants.
> (II. ii. 72–83)

The close similarity between the language and thought of this passage and Troilus' earlier comments on the mercantile nature of his pursuit of Cressida reveals the strength of the underlying metaphoric conception informing the unfolding action in the various plot strands. There is more to observe here, however, than just interesting double-plot parallelism. The subtle metaphoric cross-reference between the two actions creates a rather dazzling multi-perspective in which the dismal outcome of Troilus' anticipated attainment of Cressida is actually suggested in advance by its metaphoric association with the already completed Princes-Paris-Helen action. Why dispatch Pandarus, the juxtaposition subtly implies to us but not to Troilus, when his counterpart Paris brought home such unanticipated consequences? If Helen too was formerly a pearl, perhaps Cressida had better be left on her bed in India.

We should note that Troilus passionately refuses in this scene to abdicate responsibility for delegated actions. Whatever actions Paris has taken reflect back upon those who submitted their desires to his agency. "We turn not back the silks upon the merchant / When we have soiled them" (II. ii. 69–70), Troilus explains. Unlike the widely acclaimed Hector, Troilus at least faces directly in this debate the central issue of the play. Given the perverting nature of medium, he seems to ask, what kind of stance is acceptable? If all pearls become, in the process of attaining them, only soiled silks and "remainder viands" (both Helen and Cressida become identified with scraps of leftover food), then what recourse aside from passive despair can man have? It is clearly off the subject to expound, as Hector does to almost universal critical applause, on the laws of nature and moral laws, since he too presumably consented to Paris' mission. It is not difficult to be sententiously moral after the fact.

The imagery of buying and selling and the various strategies of salesmanship and merchandising are not simply characteristics of Troilus' speech; they color the expression of many quite different characters. Like the two plot strands observed above, for instance, the Ulysses-Ajax-Achilles plot uses the same controlling framework of merchant imagery. If Pandarus and Paris are the agents in their respective actions, Ajax becomes the middleman in this affair. "Ajax employed," Ulysses says succinctly, "plucks down Achilles' plumes" (I. iii. 385). As he broaches his scheme to Nestor, Ulysses turns naturally to the familiar merchant metaphor.

> Let us, like merchants,
> First show foul wares, and think perchance they'll sell;
> If not, the lustre of the better shall exceed
> By showing the worse first.
> (I. iii. 358–61)

The reactivation of Achilles, motionless "upon a lazy bed," is the particular "pearl" Ulysses seeks, and Ajax seems to him the proper agency through which to effect the acquisition. Again this enterprise is no more successful than the other two ventures, ending in equally total frustration. "The policy of those crafty swearing rascals," Thersites sums up near the end of the play, "is not proved worth a blackberry" (V. iv. 9–11). It is very unlikely anyway that Ulysses' salesmanship strategy would have fooled the Trojans, who are just as crafty as the Greeks in the subtleties of buying and selling. For example, Paris immediately discounts Diomedes' bitter remark on the worthlessness of Helen as merely a specious piece of low-pressure salesmanship.

Fair Diomed, you do as chapmen do,
Dispraise the thing that you desire to buy;
But we in silence hold this virtue well,
We'll not commend what we intend to sell.
(IV. i. 75–78)

By surveying the similarities and differences between the several merchant figures in *Troilus,* we can see that character analysis of a moralistic nature will not be entirely responsive to the play's vital concerns. If we accuse Troilus of a self-justifying passivity in his reliance on Pandarus, are we then willing to level the same charge at Priam's Princes for their reliance on Paris, or at Ulysses and Nestor for their use of Ajax? Ulysses is not passive; indeed, he works as hard as he can to make his plan work, and yet his failure is no less complete than the others. Shakespeare seems to go to some trouble to convince his audience that all human plots—reasonable or emotional—are doomed to failure: as Sonnet 94 concludes, "sweetest things turn sourest by their deeds." To illustrate the origins of that gloomy and fatalistic attitude, Shakespeare shows us how Pandarus, Paris, and Ajax, in their actions as agents, unintentionally cheapen and pervert the aspirations that have been subjected to their instrumentation. Shakespeare does not encourage us to criticize these characters because of their inability to fulfill their assignments; instead, he directs our attention to a more radical inadequacy felt in the mediated nature of human action itself. Most importantly, the characters are forced by the requirements of the play to act within the context of an indissoluble trinity of desire, endeavor, and achievement, which, by focusing on the debilitating nature of medium, gives deep cogency to Agamemnon's assertion that "In all designs begun on earth below" hope "Fails in the promised largeness" (I. iii. 4–5).

III

One design, "begun on earth below" and therefore presumably destined also to fall short of its "promised largeness," is Shakespeare's play *Troilus and Cressida.* In what manner does the specific form of the play reflect Shakespeare's interest in the problems of mediation previously discussed? Structure and substance, of course, are united and indissoluble in reading and performance, and we should not expect to keep a consideration of theme separate from form. In fact, a discussion of several aspects of *Troilus'* structure already lies implicit in the two preceding sections: Pandarus' role in the dynamics of the plot and the formal relationship between the three plot strands. In this section, therefore, analysis of structure will be limited to an inquiry into the felt presence of an unresponsive medium in the moving surface and linguistic texture of the play. This inquiry should help us gauge the degree to which Shakespeare senses that the recalcitrance of his medium affects his own particular artistic activity both as creator and mediator of the received mythic materials.

Several commentators have complained that the shaping impulse in the structure of *Troilus'* plot is constantly clogged, frustrated, or misdirected as it tries to move towards coherent completion. Indeed, it often seems that the outcome of scenes or episodes does not fulfill their initial intention. The disjunctive and nonsequential nature of the play's scenario, for example, provoked Bertrand Evans to exclaim that "the corruptive disease of the world of *Troilus and Cressida* is a contagious one, catching even to the bones of dramatic structure, leaving them too infirm to support the action." [14] Evans has in mind such things as the play's seeming inability to make clear the exact reason for Achilles' stubborn inaction, since various scenes advance such contradictory causes as inordinate pride, a traitorous love for Polyxena, and even a homosexual attachment for Patroclus. Several scenes seem to wander badly from their main concerns, such as II. iii, and others get bogged down in tedious verbiage and rhetoric. Moreover, there is a rather confused sense of continuity in the jerky progression of the scenes, and the temporal synchronization of the love plot and the war plot becomes almost incomprehensible if examined too closely. Philip Edwards has also observed these, and other, structural peculiarities and decided that *Troilus* is best understood as "anti-art, because its very structure is a kind of defiance of the continuity, consequence and unity which the more usual kind of play will provide." [15] In *Troilus'* structure, as well as in its theme, "checks and disasters / Grow in the veins of actions highest reared" (I. iii. 5–6).

The most troublesome impediment to the realization of highest actions in the play is language. Not only the characters but

---

[14] Bertrand Evans, *Shakespeare's Comedies* (Oxford: Oxford Univ. Press, 1960), p. 167.

[15] Edwards, p. 97. Here again Edwards is drawing upon Ellis-Fermor's earlier assertion of artistic purpose in *Troilus'* strange structure: "For, given discord as the central theme," Ellis-Fermor declares, in her aforementioned work, "it is hard to imagine how else it should be formally reflected but in a deliberately intended discord of form also" (p. 63).

the rising form of the play itself must struggle with the frustrating resistance that the medium of words can exercise. *Troilus* repeatedly brings two people together ostensibly to exchange information. In almost all cases the outcome is a tremendous explosion of words, either in the form of pointless punning or magnificent declamation and bluster that results in a very trivial exchange of information or total misunderstanding. We observed a similar tendency in *Romeo and Juliet,* but now it has become greatly intensified and more pervasive. It takes Ulysses sixteen tortuous lines to ask Agamemnon for permission to address the Greek council (I. iii. 54–69); Aeneas and Agamemnon struggle for no fewer than forty-two lines simply to make initial contact with each other (I. iii. 215–56); Pandarus leaves Troilus in a pique after completely misunderstanding his febrile attempts to praise Cressida (I. i. 70–84); it takes Pandarus forty-eight lines to tell Cressida his silly and pointless little anecdote about the fifty-two hairs on Troilus' chin (I. ii. 113–60); Ajax beats Thersites for a full scene trying to get him to "learn me the tenor of the proclamation" and never does learn it (II. i. 1–125); Pandarus and a servant talk at cross purposes for forty lines without exchanging a dram of information (III. i. 1–40); communication at one point so completely breaks down that Ajax actually mistakes Thersites for Agamemnon (III. ii. 250–64); Aeneas and Diomedes exchange pointless oxymoronic talk for thirty-five lines before getting on with the business of exchanging the prisoners (IV. i. 1–35); Nestor greets Hector with a lengthy encomium that threatens to continue indefinitely before Ulysses mercifully interrupts and changes the subject (IV. v. 182–210); Aeneas, in particular, is so addicted to high sounding language that, like his more humorous counterparts Gratiano and Mercutio, he constantly "speaks an infinite deal of nothing." A considerable disproportion obviously exists in the play between the verbal energy expended in conversation and the results achieved, a disproportion aptly expressed metaphorically in Thersites' observation that the Greeks "will not in circumvention deliver a fly from a spider, without drawing their massy irons and cutting the web" (II. iii. 14–16). The Trojans also have verbal "massy irons," which they brandish with equal superfluity.

The sheer bulk of words contained in the above examples makes it clear that a large part of the texture of *Troilus* is made up of various kinds of linguistic mismanagement. We need to determine, however, precisely the degree to which such failure to control language indicates Shakespeare's difficulties with his medium, for serious misunderstanding on this point is common. For example, Mark Van Doren rightly observed these stylistic excesses but wrongly concluded that Shakespeare "cannot control the style" of the play. "He talks at the top of his lungs and still cannot say enough, or get the right thing said." [16] In all the above examples, however, we perceive that Shakespeare is quite aware of what is happening to language and to the attempt at communication. He sees clearly that what should be a transparent and flexible medium has become opaque and resistant, clotted with high-flown rhetoric and uncontrolled verbosity. [17] The man who wrote *Love's Labour's Lost* is not likely to forget how characters can abuse language through fatalistic or arrogantly self-aggrandizing efforts to control it.

For instance, Pandarus finally concludes his tedious anecdote about Troilus' beard: "But there was such laughing, and Helen so blushed, and Paris so chafed, and all the rest so laughed, that it passed," and Cressida replies wearily, "So let it now, for it has been a great while going by" (I. ii. 158–61). Even Ulysses concludes his great speech on degree—which also takes "a great while going by"—with the apology, "To end a tale of length . . ." (I. iii. 136), and to Aeneas' overly chivalric attempt to issue Hector's challenge Agamemnon comments: "This Troyan scorns us, or the men of Troy / Are ceremonious courtiers" (I. iii. 233–34). Achilles tries later to mimic Aeneas' fluffy style, but finally has to break off in disgust:

> Marry, this, sir, is proclaimed through all our host:
> That Hector, by the fifth hour of the sun,
> Will, with a trumpet, 'twixt our tents and Troy
> Tomorrow morning call some knight to arms
> That hath a stomach, and such a one that dare
> Maintain—I know not what; 'tis trash.
> (II. i. 116–21)

The Trojans also have an acute ear for stylistic excesses, for when Diomedes and Aeneas exchange their ridiculous oxymoronic taunts, Paris wryly remarks: "This is the most despiteful gentle greeting, / The noblest hateful love, that e'er I heard of" (IV. i. 32–33). Achilles, however, seems to have the most difficulty countenancing the high style. He dispatches Thersites to Ajax in this heavily ironic manner:

> To him, Patroclus. Tell him I humbly desire the

[16] Mark Van Doren, *Shakespeare* (New York: Henry Holt, 1939), pp. 202–03.
[17] McAlindon's remarks on this peculiar characteristic of the play should be consulted. He leaves little doubt that Shakespeare is fully aware of how characters are misusing language. See pp. 30–35.

valiant Ajax to invite the most valorous Hector to
come unarmed to my tent, and to procure safe-conduct
for his person of the magnanimous and most illustrious,
six-or-seven-times-honored captain-general of the
Grecian army, Agamemnon, et caetera.
(III. iii. 271–76)

"Et caetera" indeed! Thersites' comment on his assignment reminds us
yet again of Shakespeare's awareness that his characters often use
language as a means of non-communication: "Let me bear another
[letter] to his horse, for that's the more capable creature" (301–02).

IV

Despite such clear evidence that the dramatist exercises some
control and perspective on his characters' abuse of language, we should
not conclude that Shakespeare's concern with problems of communication is primarily satiric. Aeneas makes a fool of himself whenever he
opens his mouth, but then, how should Aeneas talk in a late Renaissance play? or Hector? What linguistic decorums apply to the dramatic
recreation of an Agamemnon, Nestor, or Troilus? We cannot resolve
the problem by thumbing through Renaissance handbooks on style,
since Agamemnon was not Essex, Nestor was not Lord Burghley,
and Troilus was not the Earl of Southampton. Nor was Shakespeare
willing to follow the lead of Ben Jonson and endow his characters with
a classically proper but antiquated and anachronistic style. Shakespeare's
historical consciousness was sufficiently developed for him to realize
that he was attempting to mediate between a complex and venerable
literary tradition and his modern audience. He must have been sensitive to the contradictory nature of the several linguistic and behavioral
models available to him from Homer through Chaucer, Lydgate, and
Caxton to his contemporary Chapman. It is patronizing pseudo-his-
toricism simply to assume that Shakespeare felt compelled to debase
Cressida and to ridicule the participants in the war because Henryson
and some contemporary hacks chose to do so. The aesthetic dilemma
Shakespeare faced was less cynical: he had to be responsive to the
dictates of his received materials, while at the same time he attempted
to create a new language for these legendary figures which would give
them authentic dramatic existence for his immediate audience. The
danger—and the temptation—was that he would inadvertently
caricature his subjects: that he would "slander" them with "terms un-

squared" (I. iii. 159) and "ridiculous and silly action" (149) such as Patroclus, a more cynical dramatist within the play, does when he satirizes the Greek high command for Achilles' amusement. We see that Shakespeare's dilemma arises from his dual role as maker and mediator: on the one hand is his integrity as a creator and on the other his allegiance to the dignity of the literary tradition on which he passes judgment.

We should not attribute the strong satiric element, which critics like O. J. Campbell have discerned in *Troilus,* to Shakespeare's slavish desire to ape Jonson and Marston, for such an interpretation confuses Shakespeare's intentions with Patroclus' intentions.[18] Instead, we should trace the play's bitterness to Shakespeare's tragic recognition that the dramatist's inevitable problem with language is similar to the inevitable human problem: man is language and mediation is the ground—the Pandar—of being. For instance, Shakespeare knows that his language actually shapes the identity of his characters, sculptures them, and makes them emerge as fully articulated beings. The disheartening implications of that knowledge appear in Patroclus' vulgar dramatization of Agamemnon and Nestor and in Achilles' enthusiastic response. "'Excellent!' 'tis Agamemnon right," he cries, "'Tis Nestor right" (I. iii. 164-70). Shakespeare makes us aware here that dramatic acts have an ontological dimension and that in mediating the reality of those literary figures to his audience he, like Patroclus, is unavoidably recreating them in the present moment. We may finally feel that only a very thin line separates the Agamemnon and the Nestor Shakespeare represents from Patroclus' brutal mimicry of them, but that margin is the difference between a cynical retreat into the satiric mode and a tragic confrontation with the aesthetic and ontological problems raised by mediation.

Sigurd Burckhardt reminds us that Shakespeare often writes "a part for himself as *deviser of the plot*"[19] as a means to comment tacitly on his extra-dramatic feelings about what he has attempted to do and how well he has succeeded. To some degree, Friar Laurence serves such a function in *Romeo and Juliet.* Patroclus partially functions in that manner in *Troilus* by expressing Shakespeare's apprehensions about the negative consequences of writing plays. A more central and instructive playwright in *Troilus* is Pandarus, who, unlike Patroclus, works industriously to create a meaningful design but fails dismally.

[18] O. J. Campbell, *Comicall Satyre and Shakespeare's "Troilus and Cressida,"* (San Marino, Calif.: The Huntington Library, 1938).
[19] Burckhardt, "How Not to Murder Caesar," *Shakespearean Meanings,* p. 16.

As a surrogate dramatist Pandarus stages the assignations between Troilus and Cressida and tells them, in part, what to think and say. As self-appointed prompter he ushers in the participants and gives them their cues. "She's making her ready," he alerts Troilus, "she'll come straight; you must be witty now" (III. ii. 28–29). Most importantly, however, in his actions as go-between he recreates the lovers' identities for one another. Like Shakespeare he both mediates and creates. "No man is the lord of anything," Ulysses admonishes Achilles, "till he communicate his parts to others" (III. iii. 115–17), and Pandarus illustrates that condition of intersubjectivity by functioning as the linguistic medium through which Troilus must "communicate his parts to" Cressida, and vice versa.

Shakespeare strategically devotes the first two scenes of the play to an illustration of the difficulties Pandarus encounters in his attempt to mediate the reality of the two lovers through descriptions. In both scenes Pandarus draws on all his linguistic resources in a sincere effort to praise one lover for the benefit of the other, but the lovers find his well-intentioned efforts inadequate to their lofty conceptions of each other. Pandarus' coarse, prosaic language comes between the lovers to cheapen and pervert their relationship, to bring it down to earth. He succinctly articulates that verbal incongruity in his attempt to praise Cressida by indecorously comparing her fairness to Helen's and her wit to Cassandra's. Finally he says in exasperation and bafflement at Troilus' growing irritation: "I speak no more than truth" (I. i. 61). Troilus' bitter rejoinder—"Thou dost not speak so much"—sharply focuses the emerging problem by pointing to Pandarus' essential inadequacy as a communicator of the parts of others. Pandarus has failed to create the style that will allow communication between those very sensitive semilegendary beings. Although his intentions are nobler, he fares no better as a playwright than does Patroclus.

Troilus' annoyance at the way Pandarus "handlest in [his] discourse" (I. i. 52) Cressida's physical attributes arises from his feeling that Pandarus' verbal profanation has debased the quality of his love. His cheapening talk recalls how Juliet's Nurse diminishes Juliet's image of Romeo. A similar apprehension largely accounts for Cressida's reticence and concern for her self-protection when she converses with Pandarus about Troilus in the second scene.[20] Cressida is reluctant to permit

[20] My understanding of Pandarus' role in these opening two scenes has been enriched by the fine analyses of Eagleton and McAlindon. Eagleton says that "Cressida's reality, for Troilus, is at first totally in the possession of Pandarus: 'I cannot come to Cressid but by Pandar.' In the next scene, Pandarus reverses the process

her love for Troilus to be stage-managed by Pandarus, and it is a mistake to take anything Cressida does or says to her uncle at face value. She remains distant and noncommittal, protecting herself from contagion with halfhearted attempts at humor as Pandarus tries to excite her with cheap and grossly inappropriate praise of Troilus: "I think his smiling becomes him better than any man in all Phrygia" (I. ii. 116–17). He ludicrously attempts to elevate Troilus in her esteem by reciting the long and stupid tale of how Cassandra and Hecuba "laughed that [their] eyes ran o'er" (I. ii. 136) at a silly joke Helen made on Troilus' beard, as if these somber archetypes of envisioned apocalypse and austere suffering were comic refuges from the drawing rooms of *Much Ado About Nothing*. We sense Cressida's attempts to keep herself untainted by his cheapening talk behind the characterless nature of her conversation. It is not until after Pandarus leaves the stage that we learn what is really on her mind.

> Words, vows, gifts, tears, and love's full sacrifice
> He offers in another's enterprise;
> But more in Troilus thousandfold I see
> Than in the glass of Pandar's praise may be.
> (I. ii. 268–71)

Cressida's words reflect back upon the peculiar action of *Troilus'* opening two scenes, confirming our uneasiness about Pandarus' communicative powers and reinforcing our suspicions that Shakespeare is presenting him as an inadequate but necessary dramatist. Troilus "cannot come to Cressid but by Pandar," and Cressida is obliged by the conditions of the play to find the image of her love for Troilus "in the glass of Pandar's praise." Cressida's metaphor is instructive, since her mirror image nicely suggests the key issue of linguistic recreation of identity and the inability of Pandarus' praise to reflect that identity without distortion and vulgarization. There is a wider application too, for if the purpose of acting is indeed to hold the mirror up to nature, Shakespeare may encourage us to hear in Cressida's comment his own note of disillusionment with the mimetic capabilities of the "glass" he holds up to nature. Yet we must not identify Shakespeare too closely with Pandarus. If he locates one important aspect of his dilemma in the dramatic

---

by describing Troilus to Cressida" (p. 14). McAlindon says, "Whatever slight chance the dialogues of the lovers might have had of developing into lyrical duets is completely eliminated by [Pandarus]. He is always present at some point, interrupting and commenting, turning poetry into prose and passion into lust" (p. 40).

failures of Pandarus and even Patroclus, he can also distance himself from the problems in the play and thus comprehend them as no one within it can. What Shakespeare does finally grasp is the very thing of which the Troy myth speaks: that the rape of Helen and the surrender of Cressida are archetypes which represent the universal flaw in all human exchange. Aesthetically, Shakespeare sees that the "first" war (Greeks against the Trojans) and the "first" infidelity (Cressida's betrayal of Troilus) are best understood as metaphors, of which all subsequent wars and infidelities in the literary tradition are imperfect repetitions. What is strikingly unique about *Troilus* is the degree to which Shakespeare comprehends and dramatizes the artist's inescapable condition as mediator. To acknowledge that achievement is to see *Troilus and Cressida* as it has always been: a crucial moment in Shakespeare's gradual discovery of his medium and his own limited powers over it.

III RAGOZINE'S HEAD

Comic Solutions Through Fraudulent Mediation in *Measure for Measure*

❧

Put not yourself into amazement how these things should be; all difficulties are but easy when they are known. (IV. ii. 195–97)

Shakespeare, C. L. Barber reminds us, "has an Elizabethan delight in extremes for their own sake, beyond the requirements of his form, and sometimes damaging to it." [1] In his most successful plays he disciplines that proclivity for damaging extremes with an answering delight, no less Elizabethan, in the articulation of planes of reality designed to reconcile seemingly disjunctive perspectives. Shakespeare's love of human diversity, aided by his unparalleled powers of compression, counterbalances the inclusive reach of his vision and makes possible its realization in the form of poetic drama.

Our studies of *Romeo and Juliet* and *Troilus and Cressida,* however, have suggested that there are occasions when Shakespeare feels more compelled to dramatize his sensitivity to the divisive tendencies in his complex medium than to celebrate its harmonizing capabilities. In *Romeo* we observed how Shakespeare arranged for his medium partially to decompose into the simpler components of words and actions and then revealed, through their dramatized inadequacies, the failure of both those agencies to mediate the extreme dualities of that polarized play-world. In *Troilus'* peculiar artistry we found a desire to focus attention on the creator's gloomy realization that his medium may

---

[1] C. L. Barber, *Shakespeare's Festive Comedy: A Study of Dramatic Form and its Relation to Social Custom* (Princeton: Princeton Univ. Press, 1959), p. 237.

at times appear to resist his efforts to achieve a full articulation of form and meaning. Although the concerns of these plays, as we have analyzed them, may strike some as rather uncharacteristic of Shakespeare's genius, it is probably his willingness to undertake such experimental probes into the nature of the dramatic medium that makes possible the astonishing orchestrations of language and action in *Hamlet, Othello,* and *King Lear.* It may be significant in this regard that each of those masterpieces is closely allied with one of his supposed failures in formal construction: *Hamlet* with *Troilus and Cressida, Othello* with *Measure for Measure,* and *King Lear* with *Timon of Athens.* These odd couplings imply that Shakespeare's gradual mastery of his art did not proceed by a steady and confident growth in talent but rather through disruptive periods of radical inquiry, during which he discovered the rich potentialities of his medium through controlled violations of its synthesizing powers.

I

Measure for Measure is a particularly instructive example of such bold and damaging experimentation, for no other Shakespearean play appears more willfully to sabotage its own magnificent promise of artistic unity and thematic coherence. It can disappoint and exasperate its audience more than either *Troilus* or *Timon* because, unlike those plays, it so convincingly demonstrates in its first two acts an ability that it subsequently fails to sustain. The more we respond to the formal brilliance and psychological penetration of those scenes, the less we agree with those critics who say they find the play satisfactorily unified. The price of such unity is a willingness to diminish the turbulent vitality and dramatic immediacy of the play's first half. A more fruitful approach may be that taken by such recent commentators as E. M. W. Tillyard, A. P. Rossiter, Marco Mincoff, and Philip Edwards,[2] whose

---

[2] "One of the prime facts," Tillyard says of *Measure for Measure,* is "that the play is not of a piece but changes its nature halfway through." E. M. W. Tillyard, *Shakespeare's Problem Plays* (London: Chatto & Windus, 1950), p. 123. Rossiter says that "it is to me quite evident that the texture of the writing—the denseness of image and evocative quality—undergoes an abrupt change when the Duke begins talking prose in III. i.; and that this change applies more or less to all the *serious* matter thereafter." A. P. Rossiter, *Angel With Horns* (New York: Theatre Arts, 1961), p. 164. "We are thoroughly cheated," Edwards says of the play after the Duke's intervention, and he goes on to assert that the play "can only be kept heartwhole by methodical criticism which treats it as an allegory, which it certainly is not." Philip Edwards, *Shakespeare and the Confines of Art* (London:

detailed analyses lead them to the conviction that the two distinctively different halves of the play are not compatible and that the second half is lamentably inferior in quality to the first: a troubling conclusion, perhaps, but one more responsive to our emotional and intellectual involvement in the play.

We can pinpoint our sense of a fundamental disjunction in the play's organization with unusual exactness. It arises as the immediate consequence of the stunning moment during Act III, scene 1 when Duke Vincentio, disguised as a friar, steps out of the shadows that have enveloped him during most of the play's early action and calmly proceeds to take over the full management of his people's hopelessly stalemated lives. "Fasten your ear on my advisings," he orders the distraught Isabella, "to the love I have in doing good a remedy presents itself" (III. i. 194–95). The objectifying passivity asserted by the Duke's "fasten your ear" image is prophetically apt, for his inadequately motivated act of intervention will transform every element of the play, from small stylistic units to large patterns of theme and characterization. Through his abrupt offer of a remedy, programmed to rescue his impassioned subjects from their respective dilemmas, the Duke-Friar cancels, in effect, the dynamics of the first two acts and superimposes upon it a new pattern of relationships conveniently open to a rather simple solution. Moreover, Shakespeare makes little effort to blur the edges be-

---

Methuen, 1968), pp. 117; 119. Mincoff comments on "the loss of vitality in the second half" and adds that "surely no great play—for it is a great play as it begins— loses itself so lamentably in the sands as this. . . . it is almost sheer dead weight." Marco Mincoff, *"Measure for Measure:* A Question of Approach," *Shakespeare Studies,* 2 (1966), pp. 145–46. This general feeling that there is a damaging break in the play, however, was set forth earlier by L. C. Knights who observed that "the last two acts, showing obvious signs of haste, are little more than a drawing out and resolution of the plot." "The Ambiguity of *Measure for Measure,*" *Scrutiny,* 10 (1942), p. 232. Herbert Weil, Jr., in a more recent essay, calls attention to "the extreme shift in subject matter, style, and tone at that moment—Act III, scene i, line 152—when the Duke interrupts Isabella's outburst against her brother." "Form and Contexts in *Measure for Measure,*" *Critical Quarterly,* 12 (1970), p. 56. The critics who find the play perfectly unified are best represented by F. R. Leavis who answered Knights' charges of disjunction by stating: "My own view is clean contrary: it is that the resolution of the plot of *Measure for Measure* is a consummately right and satisfying fulfillment of the essential design." "The Greatness of *Measure for Measure,*" *Scrutiny,* 10 (1942), p. 243. Among more recent critics to take the Leavis line of approach is David L. Stevenson, *The Achievement of Shakespeare's "Measure for Measure"* (Ithaca, N. Y.: Cornell Univ. Press, 1966), who argues that *"Measure for Measure* is a brilliant, self-contained artistic achievement which carries its meaning within its own dramatic design" (p.5).

tween those rather awkwardly juxtaposed planes of representation. Instead, he leaves character, theme, action, and language standing in slightly opaque relationship to each other. Hence, only the most determined exponents of organic unity can make fully consistent personalities of the major characters who appear in both halves.

The two plays we have previously examined provide antecedents for understanding the peculiar role Duke Vincentio assumes once his conciliatory gesture locates him at the center of the play's action. His offer to serve as a busy intermediary aligns him, on the one hand, with Pandarus the bustling go-between in *Troilus*, and, on the other, with Friar Laurence the harassed arbitrator in *Romeo*.[3] Indeed, part of our difficulty in assessing the Duke's character is traceable to the composite nature of his dramatic image: part friar, part bawd. Despite his disclaimers, he implicitly allies himself with the bawd and his "hold-door trade" through his management of the shady, clandestine arrangements to slip Mariana into Angelo's bed. His friar's habit, combined with his willingness to intervene on behalf of young lovers facing imminent death (one of whom is named Juliet), associates him with *Romeo*'s well-intentioned friar. In addition, both those benevolent friars only come into prominence during the second halves of their plays, where their desperately revised schemes are closely synchronized with the plays' episodic actions. However, Friar Laurence's mediation ends in abject failure and tragic death, whereas the Duke-Friar's intervention leads, with only some minor setbacks, to unqualified success and the anticipation of multiple marriages. Still, the difference may not be so great as it seems, for the manipulation and strain required to bring off the happy ending suggest that the Duke-Friar's intervention produces a comic conclusion in the technical sense more than in the aesthetic and thematic sense. That is, his assertion of control does rescue the characters from impending disaster but simultaneously diminishes them as freestanding and dynamic personalities. Here again the disguised Duke reminds us of Pandarus, in that both those agents arrange successfully for a full satisfaction of desire but in the very process seem inadvertently

---

[3] W. W. Lawrence was one of the first critics to notice the similarity between the role Duke Vincentio assumes and that of Friar Laurence in *Romeo*. "Shakespeare was here merely repeating a device which he had already used more than once, whereby an ecclesiastic straightens out the complications of a difficult situation, and by his spiritual authority gives confidence and sanction to the execution of a ruse—Friar Laurence in *Romeo and Juliet*, Friar Francis in *Much Ado*." *Shakespeare's Problem Comedies* (New York: Macmillan, 1931), p. 92.

to debase and cheapen the desired object. What the Duke leaves us with both "is, and is not" what we had hoped for. As the action moves towards its inevitable resolution under his firm guidance we may perhaps hear faint echoes from an earlier occasion of well-meaning but deadly mediation: "Why the devil came you between us? I was hurt under your arm" (*Romeo*. III. i. 100–01). At any rate, to see *Measure for Measure* against the background of *Romeo* and *Troilus* is to see it as another instance of Shakespeare's exploratory concern with processes of imperfect mediation.

Shakespeare's decision to allow the ambiguous Duke-Friar to commence arbitrating the difficulties facing Claudio, Isabella, and Angelo irreversibly commits his play-world to an apparently endless supply of increasingly fraudulent mediators. Once the disguised Duke intercedes, he quickly spawns a number of new figures whose only reason for dramatic existence is to step into the vacant space between deadlocked extremes in order to function as a mediating third term. Even the characters formerly occupying those rigid defenses are rather clumsily re-positioned by Shakespeare so as to insure a successful mediation of differences. Isabella, formerly an independent and authentic personality with a voice of her own, is suddenly reduced to little more than a willing adjunct to the Duke's purpose; Angelo is also degraded and furnished with a new and ill-fitting past history; and Claudio simply vanishes as a viable dramatic entity.[4] Those necessary maneuvers completed, Shakespeare introduces Mariana, Angelo's abandoned fiancée, as a convenient substitute for Isabella in Angelo's bed, thereby dissolving with one stroke the basic conflict of the first two acts.[5] To sustain a degree of dramatic tension, however, he has the lust-sated Angelo still refuse to pardon Claudio, forcing the inventive Duke-Friar to bring into existence yet another substitute to die in Claudio's place. That new character, Barnardine, carries impeccable credentials for a summary beheading, but Shakespeare wonderfully endows him with too much creaturality and comic integrity to serve as a stand-in for someone else's

---

[4] Tillyard notes the fundamental change in Isabella's representation and charges that "she has been turned into a mere tool of the Duke" (p. 129). J. W. Lever, in his fine "Introduction" to The New Arden Shakespeare edition of *Measure for Measure* (Cambridge, Mass.: Harvard Univ. Press, 1965), comments that "the other main figures lose much of their independent volition" after the Duke's takeover (p. xcv).

[5] Mincoff complains that by substituting Mariana for Isabella "the initial hypothesis of the play is nonchalantly discarded, and one feels that the issue has been shirked and one's emotions tricked out of one" (p. 146).

execution. This funny incident calls attention to the increasingly disingenuous nature of the play's determination to mediate all problems no matter what the cost in credibility. After being momentarily stalled by Barnardine's stubbornness, the action is suddenly propelled forward to its *reductio ad absurdum* with the astonishingly sophistical introduction of a dramatic nonentity called Ragozine, whom Shakespeare simply conjures out of thin air to supply the head needed to keep Claudio's in place.[6] No Shakespearean play pivots on a more insubstantial peg than that provided by Ragozine's head: a middle term of remarkable nullity. The Duke's pious exclamation on learning of this crude piece of theatrical chicanery—"O, 'tis an accident that heaven provides" (IV.iii.74)— resonates with Shakespearean skepticism and gentle self-mockery. Other lesser agents will also make their assigned contributions to the Act V denouement (such as the Provost and Friar Peter), but the ludicrous recourse here to Ragozine's head surely pushes the pattern of specious mediation to a vanishing point where the whole pretense of an effective arbitration of human problems threatens to dissolve in laughter and disbelief. Although the play's happy ending depends entirely on the finely coordinated actions of the Duke and his sub-mediators, not one of them, on a spectrum stretching from the Duke to Ragozine, really convinces us of his legitimacy.

Despite such an infinite proliferation of available middlemen —or perhaps because of them—there is no real sense of operative mediation in *Measure for Measure*. As a result, we encounter everywhere in the play's structure a disjunction of vision and purpose: an obsession with contrarieties which cannot be resolved in any comprehensive overview.[7] Shakespeare gives two incompatible reasons for the Duke's sudden departure; two quite different men are deputized to replace him; Claudio voices two opposed reasons for his arrest; Pompey and Claudio furnish two contrary examples of Viennese justice; two meetings occur between Angelo and Isabella; two women engage in premarital sex (Juliet's is condemned, Mariana's sanctioned); two very dissimilar men await execution in the prison; characters defend two disjunct ethical systems; and there are allusions to two radically differ-

---

[6] Weil has some fine remarks on the humorous disbelief generated by this pattern of substitution in the play. "The sequence of substitutions through which Vincentio saves Claudio becomes progressively more farfetched. . . . Even if [the spectator] has somehow taken quite earnestly the Duke's plans for the substitution of Mariana, the second and third ready-made substitutions would strain his belief. They clearly push too far an initially shaky plot device" (pp. 60–61).

[7] Rossiter, p. 164.

ent Biblical codes of behavior in the very title of the play—a title which is itself a doublet. The play's clear intent is "to unfold the properties of government" (a slight rearrangement of the opening line), but it does so by generating sets of antitheses that exclude an accommodating middle.

The play's inability to resolve unmediated extremes is most disturbing, however, in its presentation of single characters. We are asked to believe that the major characters undergo crucial changes, but critics have been unable to trace the stages of transition that would make such character development understandable. For example, Leo Kirschbaum discovers "two strikingly disparate characterizations" of Angelo in the play and is forced to conclude that "it is impossible to bring the two divergent portrayals together."[8] L. C. Knights and A. P. Rossiter find a similar uncertainty and doubleness in the presentation of Claudio and Angelo; indeed, Rossiter can find unity of being only in the single-minded Barnardine.[9] However, it is the Duke himself who has most disappointed commentators in search of integrated personality and synthesizing action. We expect that the Duke's intervention will function thematically to mediate the rigid polarities of justice and mercy, and that his decisions will finally moderate those ethical absolutes into some pattern of acceptable compromise. But Mincoff's rigorous scrutiny of the play's ideas demonstrates fairly convincingly that the Duke (and the play) "merely vacillates" between full adherence to one view and full adherence to the other.[10] Of course, we cannot deny that the Duke's Fifth Act extravaganza achieves a dramatic solution of sorts, but, as Rossiter succinctly puts it, "the 'problem' is on one plane, the 'solution' on quite another."[11]

Discontinuity appears even in the relation between character and speech. Arthur Sewell charts the psychic continuum between Angelo and his ego-shattering discovery of inner corruption and discerns a hiatus between expression and fact. "There is always a separateness between Angelo and his lust; and the lust is simple and opaque . . . to the earlier nature of the man." The language of Angelo's introspection, Sewell notes, "scarcely ever reveals the darker recesses

[8] Leo Kirschbaum, "The Two Angelos" in *Character and Characterization in Shakespeare* (Detroit, Mich: Wayne State Univ. Press, 1962), pp. 119, 120.
[9] Knights finds "a slight uncertainty of attitude in Shakespeare's handling of [Claudio]," and says "that explains some part, at least, of the play's disturbing effect" (p. 225). Rossiter, pp. 163, 166.
[10] Mincoff, p. 150.
[11] Rossiter, p. 169.

of his being; nothing rises from the center. . . . This is not appetite speaking, but the man about the appetite." [12] Sewell's comments may remind some of Sir Arthur Quiller-Couch's conviction that the speech of Isabella and the Duke in "the two halves of [Act III, scene 1] cannot be made of a piece by anyone possessing even a rudimentary acquaintance with English prose or poetry."[13] However, Rossiter gives those particular insights more application when he declares "the whole play is full of equivocal speeches, of the kind where there is no resolving the ambiguities." [14] He traces the play's disjunctive vision to smaller linguistic patterns, such as the recurrent reliance on phrasal doublets (e.g., "Mortality and mercy in Vienna / Live in thy tongue and heart" [I. i. 44–45]), and concludes that such locutions suggest "a mind taken up with the complexity—and contradictariness—of experience: trying to force as much as possible of it into double epithets or verbs with an abrupt change of aspect." [15] Finally, William Empson, working brilliantly at the most minute level of stylistic analysis, follows the use of the complex word "sense" through the play and finds it impossible to reconcile its exclusive meanings. "The equations can be made to give a variety of minor doctrines," he decides, "but it is not clear how well they hang together. . . . It seems to me another case of the incomplete double symbol." [16]

Like Isabella, "at war 'twixt will and will not" (II. ii. 33), or Angelo, fixed at the juncture "Where prayers cross" (II. ii. 159), *Measure for Measure* is racked by fundamental division. The preceding analyses are valuable because their rigorous attention to detail is rare in the burgeoning commentary (mostly Bradleian or allegorical) on the play and because they all point to a conclusion of sizable importance. From general considerations of plot and character to the detailed inspections of syntax and semantics, they reveal the work of an artist who obstinately refuses, or perhaps is temporarily unable, to admit into his play any valid form of the mediate. By momentarily abandoning that rich middle ground where contraries can meet legitimately (i.e., without recourse to Ragozine's head), Shakespeare seems determined

[12] Arthur Sewell, *Character and Society in Shakespeare* (Oxford: Oxford Univ. Press, 1951), p. 70.

[13] Sir Arthur Quiller-Couch, "Introduction," to his New Cambridge edition of the play (Cambridge: Cambridge Univ. Press, 1922), p. xxxix.

[14] Rossiter, p. 163.

[15] Ibid., p. 164.

[16] William Empson, *The Structure of Complex Words* (London: Chatto & Windus, 1951), p. 287. See also the entirety of the excellent chapter entitled "Sense in *Measure for Measure*," pp. 270–88.

to project into the play his troubled awareness of the disjunctive propensities in both art and human experience. The following sections will explore this hypothesis.

II

The first half of *Measure for Measure* is obsessed with the ways language, conceived as the medium through which man's existence in a community becomes possible, can be discredited as an instrument for purposive human action. What primarily necessitates the play's acquiescence into disjunction and varieties of specious mediation is Shakespeare's insistent dramatization in the early scenes of the total breakdown of language as an effective means of interpersonal communication. Hence, social relationships appear from the outset as regressing away from the mediating institutions of society back into a more immediate and isolating contact with nature. Such a regression implies a withdrawal from an unmanageable word-medium in favor of a direct encounter with things. Duke Vincentio's hasty leave-taking, his shy avoidance of the "loud applause and aves vehement" (I. i. 70) of his subjects, and his reluctance "t'affect speech and discourse" (I. i. 4) in his delegation of authority, underscore at once the play's concern with the bond between language and society.

Claudio and Juliet occupy the center of the play's focus on social discourse, and in their technically lawless and secret cohabitation they represent a fundamental violation of the mediating terms society imposes between desire and gratification. We can easily diminish the play into melodrama unless we grasp the crucial point that the lovers have not just ignored some silly local ordinance but have innocently denied the humanizing function of the word. Claudio's own explanation of his act and its consequences unfolds its symbolic scope.

> You know the lady, she is fast my wife
> Save that we do the denunciation lack
> Of outward order. This we came not to,
> Only for prorogation of a dower
> Remaining in the coffer of her friends,
> From whom we thought it meet to hide our love
> Till time had made them for us. But it chances
> The stealth of our most mutual entertainment
> With character too gross is writ on Juliet.
> (I. ii. 142–50)

The extenuating circumstances have only a surface importance and, in fact, are never mentioned in defense of the lovers. What counts is that the lovers, in their desire for the immediacy of a "most mutual entertainment," have elected to bypass the prescribed medium of social language ("the denunciation . . . Of outward order") and as a result have inadvertently fallen victim to another more primitive mode of expression. Their marginal capitulation to natural impulse finds unmediated expression in the revelatory language of Juliet's visible pregnancy—a communication inscribed "With character too gross" to escape detection.

"All cultural work," Ernst Cassirer writes, "proceeds by the gradual shift from the direct relation between man and his environment to an indirect relation."[17] In linguistic terms that means the word is gradually liberated from bondage to the immediate appearance of things and allowed to assume a mediating position between man and his desires. We evolve a social language in order to identify our desires by distancing ourselves from impulses that are, if pursued directly, unnameable. "In the beginning," Cassirer says of this civilizing process, "sensual impulse is followed immediately by its gratification; but gradually more and more mediating terms intervene between the will and its object."[18] By ignoring those mediating terms, Claudio and Juliet suggest how culture, with its generative linguistic component, can be readily collapsed back into a mute state of nature. Shakespeare beautifully underscores that point in the images he gives to Lucio, when he describes to Isabella the consequences of the lovers' intercourse.

> Your brother and his lover have embraced;
> As those that feed grow full, as blossoming time
> That from the seedness the bare fallow brings
> To teeming foison, even so her plenteous womb
> Expresseth his full tilth and husbandry.
> (I. v. 40–44)

[17] Ernst Cassirer, *Language and Myth,* trans. Suzanne K. Langer (New York: Dover, 1953), p. 58. First published in 1917 in Germany as *Sprache und Mythos.*
[18] Ibid., p. 58. On this subject Paul de Man writes: "We know that our entire social language is an intricate system of rhetorical devices designed to escape from the direct expression of desires that are, in the fullest sense of the term, unnameable—not because they are ethically shameful (for this would make the problem a very simple one), but because unmediated expression is a philosophical impossibility." *Blindness and Insight: Essays in the Rhetoric of Contemporary Criticism* (Oxford: Oxford Univ. Press, 1971), p. 9.

The lines are deceptively lovely, for they give eloquent testimony to our perennial dream of a pastoral state of nature that will accommodate our desire. Lucio's two similes associate free sexuality first with a full satisfaction of appetite ("As those that feed grow full") and then with the natural spontaneous fecundity of inseminated earth. We clearly see the positive attractions of pregnancy as "blossoming time," but we also see that those satisfactions are closely linked with a full capitulation to the immediate language of nature. It is Juliet's "plenteous womb" that "Expresseth [Claudio's] full tilth and husbandry." The verb "express" carries the usual Shakespearean meaning of "to manifest or reveal," but it also activates the more precise Latinate notion of "pressing forth." [19] The pun on burgeoning bellies as a form of speechless confession suggests that Shakespeare's concern here is with the way the realm of the uniquely human can give way to nonverbal natural processes. In this regard it is probably significant that Juliet speaks only nine lines in the play and that Claudio is almost totally mute in the second half: their silent presence is their chosen mode of being. Likewise, the Duke arranges Angelo's sexual encounter with Mariana, which parallels the lovers, to occur in a "time [that] may have all shadow and silence in it" (III. i. 240–41). In both cases satisfaction of personal desire is associated with stealth and silence.

The Angelo we meet in the play's first half, however, stands at the opposite extreme from the lovers in the play's dialectic, since he functions as spokesman for the absolute efficacy of language. As the deputy informs Isabella, he is "the voice of the recorded law" (II. iv. 61) in Vienna: it is his "proclamation" that plucks down the disease-ridden whorehouses, and it is "surely for a name" (I. ii. 166) that he imprisons and condemns Claudio. In him the word of civil discourse becomes law—abstract, impersonal, and inviolate—and, as such, creates an ideal of secular culture which the people of the play cannot live up to. Angelo's "settled visage and deliberate word," as Isabella puts it, "Nips youth i' th' head" (III. i. 90–91); his dedication to "follow close the rigor of the statute" (I. iv. 67) threatens the very life of Vienna. In fact, the play's criticism of the lovers for their surrender to sensual impulse (not very severe in the first place) is further qualified by the unattractive quality of Angelo's verbal absolutism. Shakespeare uses the clear opposition between Angelo and the

---

[19] The *Oxford English Dictionary* lists the Latinate notion of "pressing forth" as the primary meaning of "express," but it is clear that the present meaning of the word was also available to Shakespeare. It is a complex word worthy of the attention of Empson.

lovers to suggest that the natural language of the body and the articulate language of the mind are mutually incompatible in this play,
and that the latter must inevitably give way to the former.

Two expressive organs, Juliet's womb and Angelo's tongue,
appear as opposed media for human intercourse in *Measure*. The
dynamic tension arising from this stark duality is focused most sharply
in Isabella, who is aligned with both the deputy and the lovers. We
meet her as she is about to enter the convent, and we hear the play's
most explicit statement of its polarized communicative medium as
Nun Francisca tersely describes to Isabella the peculiar decorum
required of novices.

> When you have vowed, you must not speak with men
> But in the presence of the prioress;
> Then, if you speak, you must not show your face,
> Or, if you show your face, you must not speak.
> (I. iv. 10–13)

The syllogistic precision of this command suggests that Isabella will
live the division that severs Angelo's word from Juliet's body. Her
future contacts with men will be through one of two isolated media:
she can speak her mind or show her face, but not both. Nun Francisca's
harsh disjunction recalls Hamlet's brutal advice to Ophelia that "your
honesty should admit no discourse to your beauty" (*Hamlet*. III. i. 107–
08). In both cases the survival of human values (speech and honesty)
is made dependent upon a total segregation of mind from body. Hamlet's reason for ordering Ophelia to "get thee to a nunnery" (121)
is his conviction that "the power of beauty will sooner transform
honesty from what it is to a bawd than the force of honesty can trans-
late beauty into his likeness" (111–13). Because of this imbalance favoring
the corrupting power of beauty, there must be no communication between it and honesty. Isabella's proposed entry into the nunnery is a
radical gesture calculated to keep her from becoming "a breeder of
sinners" (122) like her "cousin" Juliet. Only within the schizoid world
of the convent is it possible to keep the opposed modes of discourse
(language and nature) separate and equal. However, the possibility
remains only hypothetical, since Shakespeare refuses her the sanctuary
of the convent and compels her to act in the debased public world of
Vienna where beauty, as Hamlet had warned, does insidiously corrupt
the honest language of the mind.

What endangers the efficacy of words is the mute but powerfully expressive presence of the erotic body. We quickly see just why

the curious rule against both speaking and showing the face makes sense in the world of *Measure* when Isabella appears before Angelo in the great debate scenes of Act II. Indeed, the subtle dynamics of those scenes cannot fully be understood unless we are alert to the play of crosscurrents generated by the discrepancy between the speaking mind and the speaking body.[20] Here again Shakespeare carefully prepares the way in which we should view these *agons* between man and woman. Even before we meet Isabella at the nunnery we hear Claudio describe in very precise terminology his sister's dual powers of persuasion. "Acquaint her with the danger of my state," he tells his friend Lucio.

> Implore her, in my voice, that she make friends
> To the strict deputy; bid herself assay him.
> I have great hope in that; for in her youth
> There is a prone and speechless dialect,
> Such as move men; beside, she hath prosperous art
> When she will play with reason and discourse,
> And well she can persuade.
> (I. ii. 174–81)

The sexual overtones in "bid herself assay him" suggest the sort of rhetoric Claudio believes has the better chance of saving his head. Isabella's youth and lovely femininity speak an irresistible language of the body that will instinctively move men. On the other hand, she has cultivated the art of public speaking and is adept at manipulating words ("play with reason and discourse") in order to debate persuasively. However, Claudio's words emphasize the disjunction between the naturally acquired "prone and speechless dialect" and the cunningly learned "prosperous art," and he strongly hints at the superiority of her natural gifts over her artful ones. Moreover, the striking use of "prone," in close association with "speechless dialect" and with its erotic connotations of inviting passivity, seems calculated to relate the chaste Isabella to the sexual mode of discourse Juliet represents.

The much discussed debates between Angelo and Isabella are not particularly difficult on the thematic or allegorical level: absolute Law confronts absolute Mercy and neither budges an inch from the extreme. As the spokesman for Mercy Isabella naturally has the most

---

[20] Lever has some insight into these tensions. "Isabel's first interview with Angelo is, in conceptual terms, a 'contention' between Mercy and Justice; its dramatic effect, however, is to strain to breaking-point the tensions in Angelo's psyche" (p. xciii).

impassioned speeches, but it is, as Mincoff bluntly puts it, "cheap sentimentality" to suppose Shakespeare is really advocating the sovereignty of Mercy in those scenes.[21] The two participants seem never fully to engage on that level of abstraction; in fact, what is operative in the debates is not so much the language of reason as the provocative "speechless dialect" Claudio is banking on.[22] As Isabella gradually warms to her argument, Angelo correspondingly warms to Isabella. Shakespeare underscores that fact by situating the licentious Lucio between the two debators as a kind of perverse arbitrator. His bawdy running commentary during the first debate reveals just what Hamlet meant when he told Ophelia that the power of her beauty could transform honesty to a bawd. Lucio's remarks point with increasing explicitness to the basically erotic nature of their verbal intercourse. "You are too cold," he tells Isabella as she dispassionately begins her plea, "Give't not o'er so" (II.ii.43-45). As she gradually responds to his promptings, he encourages her further with "Ay, touch him; there's the vein" (70). The sexual basis of Isabella's appeal soon becomes undeniable in Lucio's bawdier excitations: "O, to him, to him, wench; he will relent. / He's coming, I perceive't" (124-25). Only shortly after that remark Angelo himself confesses that he has indeed succumbed, if not to her "prosperous art" then certainly to her "speechless dialect." "She speaks," he says in an aside, "and 'tis / Such sense that my sense breeds with it" (141-42). Empson has amply demonstrated how the word "sense," with its opposed meanings of sensuality and sensibleness, sustains perfectly the ambiguity between the languages of mind and body.[23] It is also important to note that the

---

[21] Mincoff, p. 150.

[22] Marion B. Smith, *Dualities in Shakespeare* (Toronto: Univ. of Toronto Press, 1966), has some useful comments on the importance of "an under-current of *double-entendre*" in Lucio's speeches, and of "the sexual ambiguities of Isabella's final plea" (pp. 144-45), but she fails to give this dynamic the full attention it deserves.

[23] Empson, p. 274. Although Empson does not mention it, there is an exchange between Nestor and Ulysses in *Troilus and Cressida* concerning Cressida's dual powers of expression that is a clear intensification of the ambiguities surrounding the word sense in *Measure for Measure*. As Cressida appears in the Greek camp, Nestor says:

> *Nestor.* A woman of quick sense.
> *Ulysses.* Fie, fie upon her!
>   There's language in her eye, her cheek, her lip;
>   Nay, her foot speaks. Her wanton spirits look out
>   At every joint and motive of her body. (*Troilus.* IV.v. 54-57)

The difference between Cressida and Isabella is that Cressida succumbs helplessly

erotic meaning is threatening to engulf the more abstract. The same imbalance is present in the question Angelo puts to himself as Isabella leaves him.

> What, do I love her,
> That I desire to hear her speak again,
> And feast upon her eyes?
> (II. ii. 177–79)

The coordinating conjunction "and" makes a futile attempt to mediate mutually exclusive responses to Isabella's petition, recalling Nun Francisca's earlier instructions about how Isabella, once safely in the nunnery, must not both speak and show her face. This brilliant scene ends with Angelo musing over Isabella's strangely erotic charms and confessing that they have conquered him, whereas "the strumpet / With all her double vigor, art and nature" (183–84) never could move him. In the phrase "double vigor, art and nature" Shakespeare perfectly encapsulates the disparate powers Isabella has exercised in her un-witting conquest of Angelo.

Angelo's soliloquy opening the scene of the second meeting makes it clear that Isabella has subdued more than just Angelo; language, too, has collapsed before the expressive appeal of the sensual body. Like Claudius in *Hamlet,* Angelo is "that way going to tempta-tion, / Where prayers cross" (II. ii. 157–58).

> When I would pray and think, I think and pray
> To several subjects: heaven hath my empty words,
> Whilst my invention [i.e., imagination], hearing not my
> tongue,
> Anchors on Isabel: heaven in my mouth,
> As if I did but only chew his name,
> And in my heart the strong and swelling evil
> Of my conception.
> (II. iv. 1–7)

---

to the image of eroticism her body presents to others, whereas Isabella resists. Still, both *Troilus* and *Measure* are structured around this radical discrepancy between the two opposed meanings of "sense." And *Troilus* may be the more honest in that it plays out the implications of this disjunctive vision to the bitter point where Troilus exclaims "This is, and is not, Cressid" (V. ii. 142), whereas *Measure* finally dissolves the discrepancy through strategies of specious mediation. Both plays are closely related in their concern for the treacherous potentialities in verbal discourse.

Between the heart and the tongue there is no reciprocal communication; the voice of one drowns out the voice of the other.[24] Angelo, the advocate of the power of words, "the voice of the recorded law," simply mouths those words which heaven expects of the tempted while simultaneously crumbling completely before the aroused appetite of the body. From this point on he uses language not substantively but only as a devious web to entrap Isabella and force her to capitulate to his lust. Isabella quickly observes that her adversary has shifted to a new style. Baffled by his riddling propositions, she pleads: "I have no tongue but one. Gentle my lord, / Let me entreat you speak the former language" (II. iv. 139–40). Angelo's former language, that medium for the expression of essential truths, has deteriorated, leaving him committed to the idiom of sensual impulse. "Nay, but hear me; / Your sense pursues not mine" (73–74), he says. "To be receivèd plain, I'll speak more gross" (82)—and he does. Gross is the appropriate term here, not only in that it emphasizes the brute physicality of Angelo's proposals, but also because it echoes Claudio's earlier description of how his surrender to sensuality "With character too gross [was] writ on Juliet." That language is now in full ascendancy in the play, so much so, in fact, that Isabella's "prosperous art" repeatedly betrays her at crucial points, leaving her increasingly vulnerable to Angelo's open aggression. When he easily points out the radical inconsistency in her expressed sense of charity, for instance, she can only utter a pathetic retraction of her whole line of argument. "O pardon me, my lord; it oft falls out / To have what we would have, we speak not what we mean" (117–18). Even her abject confessions of verbal inconsistency are made to work against her. Angelo eagerly pounces on her defensive statement of feminine frailty.

> I do arrest your words. Be that you are,
> That is, a woman; if you be more, you're none.
> If you be one, as you are well expressed
> By all external warrants, show it now,
> By putting on the destined livery.
> (II. iv. 134–38)

Isabella's theoretical arguments tend to destroy themselves through

[24] In his book *Shakespeare and Society* (New York: Schocken Books, 1967), Terence Eagleton remarks that "the image of tongue and heart recurs constantly throughout the play" (p. 76), and goes on to make some helpful observations on that feature of the play. But the heart-tongue opposition occurs in many of Shakespeare's tragedies as one element of a general vision of disjunction.

fundamental contradiction. This contradiction does not call into question her basic honesty, however; rather it reveals the treachery of a medium rapidly falling into disrepute. What does undeniably express Isabella are the "external warrants" of her body. As Angelo sees it, she may as well "put on the destined livery," since her bashful resistance only enhances her erotic appeal and further undermines the chastity her words defend. "Lay by all nicety and prolixious blushes, / That banish what they sue for" (162–63), Angelo urges her, using figurative language that sums up with amazing precision the dynamics of *Measure*'s first two acts. The shy and blushing responses of the warm-blooded virgin paradoxically speak a prolix idiom that perverts the purpose of social discourse and undermines language as a humanizing instrument. No wonder Act II ends with Isabella alone on stage declaiming against "perilous mouths" (172).

III

Angelo's abortive attempt to proclaim the efficacy of the word against the encroachments of nature results in a degeneration of his language to meaningless and hollow sounds, a mere mockery of valid communication. "Heaven hath my empty words" (II.iv.2), he admits as he gives way to "the strong and swelling evil" in his heart. Angelo's confession of linguistic impotence provides an apt approach to the several comic scenes interpolated into the first half action, for these episodes are best seen as humorous demonstrations of the close relationship in the play between sexual license and empty words. As spokesman for the crew of grotesques who provide subplot humor, Lucio accurately describes himself to Isabella as one whose "familiar sin" is "With maids to seem the lapwing and to jest, / Tongue far from heart" (I.iv.31–33). Thus, Lucio willingly lives with the same tongue versus heart dichotomy that Isabella and Angelo must passionately experience. His dismal punning match with the two Gentlemen in the play's second scene descends rapidly to silly chatter about venereal disease and fully reveals the jesting, purposeless quality of his talk. In this manner Shakespeare quickly establishes a correspondence between degrees of human depravity and degrees of linguistic debasement. When we move from the talk of Lucio and his friends to that of Mistress Overdone and her bawd Pompey, we encounter two creatures for whom even the most rudimentary discourse severely taxes their communicative powers.

MISTRESS OVERDONE. How now? What's the news with you?

POMPEY. Yonder man is carried to prison.
MISTRESS OVERDONE. Well, what has he done?
POMPEY. A woman.
MISTRESS OVERDONE. But what's his offense?
POMPEY. Groping for trouts in a peculiar river.
MISTRESS OVERDONE. What? Is there a maid with child by him?
POMPEY. No, but there's a woman with maid by him.
(I. ii. 81–89)

These characters, along with Constable Elbow and the appropriately named Froth, make up a freakish chorus of comic linguistic aberration designed to provide ironic comment, through their verbal inanity, on the more serious collapse of responsible language in the main plot. As a deformed arm of the law, for instance, Constable Elbow parodies Angelo and, through his dim-witted malapropisms, hints at the peculiar kind of reversal that awaits the judge.

The most interesting of these comic figures is Pompey, for he represents empty words at their extreme extension. Like his predecessors Mistress Quickly and Juliet's Nurse, the good-natured "tapster parcel-bawd" debases speech to a stupid and endless process of labyrinthine indirection. Language serves him as a means to evade self-incriminating communication; he can spew out great bursts of verbiage that convey nothing and go absolutely nowhere. Consider the following necessarily lengthy disquisition on the mysterious humiliation apparently inflicted on Elbow's pregnant wife by Pompey in Mistress Overdone's parlor.

> Sir, she came in great with child, and longing—saving your honor's reverence—for stewed prunes. Sir, we had but two in the house, which at that very distant time stood, as it were, in a fruit dish, a dish of some threepence; your honors have seen such dishes; they are not china dishes, but very good dishes— . . . . but to the point. As I say, this Mistress Elbow, being, as I say, with child, and being great-bellied and longing, as I said, for prunes, and having but two in the dish, as I said, Master Froth here, this very man, having eaten the rest, as I said, and, as I say . . .
> (II. i. 85–97)

Angelo, who is the target of this barrage, correctly observes "This will last out a night in Russia" (II. i. 127) and decides to abandon the case against Pompey. But Escalus presses on, advising Pompey "Come, you are a tedious fool; to the purpose" (110), until he too must finally give way before Pompey's inexhaustible chatter. The episode is hilarious, of course, but it serves also to show what a boundless wasteland language becomes when uninformed by any responsibility to truth or purpose. The final disposition of the case of Elbow v. Pompey significantly represents a capitulation to mere process. "Because he hath some offenses in him that thou wouldst discover if thou couldst," Escalus tells Elbow, "let him continue in his courses till thou know'st what they are" (176–78). We need entertain no hope that such a moment will ever come for the benighted Elbow.

The speech of the subplot characters communicates, at best, a vision of corrupt humanity hopelessly immersed in its base creaturality. Thus, at infrequent moments of lucidity they can ascend to such primitive insights as Pompey's "Does your worship mean to geld and splay all the youth of the city?" (II. i. 217–18). Even here the sadistically brutal image from animal husbandry graphically illustrates the inability of those cynical characters to perceive any kind of differentiation between humanity and bestiality. Language clearly has no authentic mediating function in such a debased context, since what they say and how they say it is exactly what they essentially are. They present themselves to each other and to the audience with a palpable immediacy that impresses us as utterly naturalistic, if not entirely admirable. Since their identities are fully present in the reality of the immediate situation, they cannot be subjected to interpretation. Here again the subplot helps us to understand the main plot, for Angelo and Isabella undergo an experience that forces them to acknowledge the immediate reality of the erotic body and to relinquish an abstract allegorical role they cannot sustain. Thus, to attempt an allegorical interpretation of the first half of *Measure,* as M. C. Bradbrook does,[25] is to place the action in an abstract context it so inexorably denies. By gradually stripping language of its interpretative function, its ability to mediate between act and significance, Shakespeare forces Angelo and Isabella to face

[25] M. C. Bradbrook, "Authority, Truth, and Justice in *Measure for Measure,*" MLR, 41 (1946), 246–55. Other critics to take the high road of allegorical exegesis are Roy W. Battenhouse, "*Measure for Measure* and Christian Doctrine of Atonement," PMLA, 61 (1946), 1029–59; Nevill Coghill, "Comic Form in *Measure for Measure,*" *Shakespeare Survey,* 8 (1955), 14–26; and J. A. Bryant, Jr., *Hippolyta's View: Some Christian Aspects of Shakspeare's Plays* (Lexington, Ky.: Univ. of Kentucky Press, 1961). A good summary of this line of criticism can be found in Stevenson. See the chapter entitled "*Measure for Measure* and Theological Exegesis," pp. 93–120.

each other with the same creatural immediacy present throughout the play in the amoral clowns.

The first half of *Measure* is as brilliant an inquiry into the status of language as Shakespeare ever carried out. Its profound skepticism erodes any naive trust in the humanizing power of words and leaves us stranded on the far side of allegory and meaning. To understand the extreme, indeed terminal nature of the linguistic progression of the play is to see just how unavoidable is the sudden intervention of Duke Vincentio in Act III, scene 1. At this point, Isabella's language has lost all modulation and oscillates wildly between shrill execration and threats of silence. Her brother Claudio's ignoble pleas for life at any cost draw from her this ultimate response:

> Take my defiance,
> Die, perish. Might but my bending down
> Reprieve thee from thy fate, it should proceed.
> I'll pray a thousand prayers for thy death,
> No word to save thee.
> (III. i. 143–47)

The numerical exaggeration reminds us that language may well have lost its power to save, but it continues to offer unlimited destructive resources to one willing "to pray a thousand prayers for . . . death." Very soon Timon will embrace this offer of destruction, but for now Shakespeare staves off the misanthrope's curses by allowing the disguised Duke to step forward and seize control of the play's action. It seems appropriate that he should do so in a linguistic context: "Vouchsafe a word, young sister, but one word" (III. i. 152). The entire play is now pivoting from tragedy to comedy on that brief but terrible silence between Isabella's "No word to save thee" and the Duke's auspicious "a word . . . but one word." One linguistic order has culminated in negation and futility; now a new order is coming into existence around the creative power of the Duke's *logos*. His triumph, however, will require a radical shift to a different medium: one that will seriously affect not only the principal characters but the play's very mode of being.

IV

That the Duke requests "but one word" suggests how fundamentally different the play is to become after his abrupt intervention. Under his guidance the action will no longer proceed through the treacherous mediacy of ambiguous discourse but through the agency of an omnipotent overseer. Duke Vincentio has the capability and godlike reason to look before and after with a glance that both sees and creates a new patterned reality in the play. His single, initiating word abolishes the temporal process dominant up to now and substitutes for it a spatial pattern of new relationships. Hence, the plot will not really develop after this point, but will simply exfoliate from the germinating word uttered by the potent Duke. Onto the stalemated situation before him, which lacks the clear outlines of a narrative, the Duke imposes a single *mythos,* a story whose life is not in its words but in its supra-linguistic *telos.* For instance, when the Duke advises Mariana that Isabella "hath a story ready for your ear" (IV. i. 55), we know *we* are not going to hear this conversation because the ready-made story can only be a further amplification of the Duke's all-embracing word. We can only regret that the encounter did not occur in the vanquished world of the first two acts where it would undoubtedly have created some verbal excitement.

The Duke's long initial address to Isabella in Act III, scene 1 best reveals the formal nature of his remedial word. His speech is full of long syntactical constructions which strain mightily to concentrate all strands of his complex story into one inclusive utterance. Notice, for example, how temporal events are first spaced out and then contracted into a single statement in this representative passage:

> I do make myself believe that you may most uprighteously
> do a poor wronged lady a merited benefit, redeem your
> brother from the angry law, do no stain to your own gracious
> person, and much please the absent Duke, if peradventure he
> shall ever return to have hearing of this business.
> (III. i. 196–201)

His retrospective summaries of past events are even more static and compressed, however, as evidenced by his account of the complicated Mariana-Angelo affair (III. i. 204–25). Those encompassing perspectives on past and future occurrences move us away from close involvement with the characters and encourage us to observe the unfolding action *sub specie aeternitatis.*[26] The panoramic nature of the Duke's speech

---

[26] Whenever a playwright shifts from dialogue and action (or scenic presentation) to narrative, we necessarily find ourselves momentarily distanced from the immediate events. However, Shakespeare uses that kind of narrative distancing for a more fundamental and permanent reorientation of our response to the action of *Measure for Measure* than we normally expect to find.

is perhaps even more obvious in his increasingly awkward and lengthy instructions to Isabella.

> This being granted in course [i.e., the assignation with Angelo]—and now follows all—we shall advise this wronged maid [Mariana] to stead up your appointment, go in your place. If the encounter acknowledge itself hereafter, it may compel him [Angelo] to her recompense; and here, by this is your brother saved, your honor untainted, the poor Mariana advantaged, and the corrupt deputy scaled.
> (III. i. 242–48)

Isabella's response to that repetitive explanation—"The image of it gives me content already, and I trust it will grow to a most prosperous perfection" (252–53)—focuses attention on the way in which the Duke's single word is now driving the play's action onward to its resolution in "most prosperous perfection."

We should note several other important points about the clumsy nature of the Duke's exposition. In length and quality it is curiously reminiscent of the long-winded prattle Pompey uses to defend himself in his Act II trial. However, Pompey takes what we suppose is a very simple story and expands it to such monstrous proportions that it never gets told; whereas the Duke takes an extremely complex story and compresses it into a barely comprehensible outline. Pompey's speech bogs down in process, while the Duke's speech suffers from a severe subordination of detail to an envisaged end product. Most importantly, both speakers are equally indifferent to the quality of their language, for neither has much faith in language as a medium adequate to human purpose. For the Duke, goal-oriented action takes clear priority over words, and under his control the characters no longer express themselves through the quality and utility of their speech but through their carefully orchestrated actions. The jerky syntax, the brusque and prosaic clauses, the constant sense of hurrying on in the Duke's speech here and elsewhere, suggest that it no longer much matters how one articulates his part in the unfolding drama. The only operative imperative is *to act it out*. Given this new modality, the several participants in the Duke's drama have very few lines to memorize: only gestures to perfect as they move stealthily in the dark. Thus, the Duke reminds Isabella to so arrange the assignation with Angelo "that the time may have all shadow and silence in it" (III. i. 240–41). Later Isabella tells Mariana, who is to become her stand-in in this prearranged scene, that "Little have you to say / When you depart from him but, soft and low, / 'Remember now my brother' " (IV. i. 67–69). We hear the same emphasis on silent gestures in Isabella's report to the Duke of how she and Angelo carefully rehearsed the details of the assignation.

> With whispering and most guilty diligence,
> In action all of precept [i.e., teaching by gestures], he did
> show me
> The way twice o'er.
> (IV. i. 38–40)

It is to such furtive, murmuring figures as these that the magnificently eloquent Judge and Virgin of the play's first two acts have been diminished by the Duke's reorientation of the play around action in place of language. The change is more generic than psychological.

As a surrogate playwright the Duke works to impose upon unregenerate nature the "most prosperous perfection" of art, thereby reversing the trend of the first half of the play, where art gave way to nature. Like Prospero, the ruler-playwright of *The Tempest,* his dramaturgy has a strong neoclassical bias. "The Duke's Apollonian intellect," J. W. Lever cogently observes, "resolved all conflicts in society and stilled all tumults in the soul." [27] Such Apollonian formalism, with its insistence on the three unities of time, place, and action, is noticeable in his instructions to Isabella: "Go you to Angelo, . . . Only refer yourself to this advantage: first, that your stay with him may not be long, that the time may have all shadow and silence in it, and the place answer to convenience" (III. i. 237–42). As he assumes more control of the action, the Duke's adherence to a rigid all-embracing decorum becomes even more pronounced. Proceeding "By cold gradation and well-balanced form" (IV. iii. 97), he assigns exact roles to his assembled troupe from which they are not to swerve an inch. To the well-rehearsed Friar Peter, for instance, he gives these last minute instructions:

> These letters at fit time deliver me.
> The provost knows our purpose and our plot;
> The matter being afoot, keep your instruction,

[27] Lever, p. xcvii. Lever's reference to "Apollonian intellect" suggests the basic shift I am emphasizing from the temporality of words to the spatiality of plot, as does his phrase "stilled all tumults in the soul." Lever goes on to assert that in that change "the autonomy of the individual was lost, and with it his innate right to choose as between evil and good."

And hold you ever to our special drift.
(IV. v. 1–4)

We may wonder, as these theatrical preparations go forward, what happened to the ruler who could say at the play's outset: "I love the people, / But do not like to stage me to their eyes" (I. i. 67–68)!

As the Duke's subjects willingly succumb to the devitalizing dictates of his art they "tend to behave," Lever says, "like animated puppets in furtherance of the Duke's design." [28] Only Isabella shows signs of momentary uneasiness as she surrenders her sense of integrity and autonomy. "To speak so indirectly I am loath," she complains of her assigned role in the denouement, "I would say the truth" (IV. vi. 1–2). However, her token gesture to the independent spirit of the Act II debates rings hollow in this new environment. Mariana's rejoinder— "Be ruled by him" (4)—compels Isabella's acquiescence, and both she and Mariana proceed to lose themselves completely in the respective parts prescribed by the Duke. They speak and act like programmed automatons during the skirmishes of Act V, and Angelo's description of them is quite correct. "I do perceive," he says as they attack him,

> These poor informal women are no more
> But instruments of some more mightier member
> That sets them on.
> (V. i. 233–36)

We are aware that Angelo is himself at this point the hapless "instrument" of that "mightier member" he faintly glimpses, but this realization does not qualify the truth of his perception. They are "informal women" because they have sacrificed their essential being to a rather sterile aesthetic formalism. During the final ninety lines of the play Isabella, her assigned role successfully concluded, can only stand silent on the stage, making no verbal response to either the miraculous appearance of her supposedly dead brother nor, more astonishingly, to the Duke's two proposals of marriage.[29]

---

[28] Ibid., p. xcv.

[29] Lever remarks that "in the last act Isabella's public humiliation is, no doubt, a necessary psychological purge, but her response to this is not very different in tone from the simulated rhetoric in which, under the Duke's coaching, she had previously denounced Angelo. . . . the Duke's final verdict is received with silent and general acquiescence" (p. xcv). Lever perhaps exaggerates the sense of "necessary psychological purge" in Isabella's final speeches, which seem to me pure theater, but his sense that we are not observing here the real Isabella of the first two acts seems accurate.

To see the Duke as a surrogate playwright is to suggest some kinship between him and Shakespeare. From the moment the Duke steps forward in Act III until he concludes the play, however, Shakespeare maintains a critical distance between himself as creator of *Measure for Measure* and the Duke as director of the play within the play. His critical detachment allows him to gauge the degree to which the Duke's dramatic achievement necessitates a harsh suppression of vital human nature. As Isabella hurries away from prison at the end of III, i to initiate the Duke's plot, for example, Shakespeare leaves the disguised ruler on stage so he can encounter all the degenerate subplot characters who are suddenly hustled into the prison. A general incarceration of Vienna low life is required to insure the aesthetic triumph the Duke envisages. After Elbow, Pompey, Lucio, and even Mistress Overdone arrive in the jail, Pompey addresses the audience on the theme of how "all great doers in our trade" (IV. iii. 17) have been forced into prison also. The long comic scenes intervene between the Duke's initial exposition and the actual performance of his plot and, therefore, reveal a degree of amused skepticism and disengagement on Shakespeare's part regarding the Duke-Friar-Dramatist's efforts to use a disciplined art to impose order on fallen humanity. Such skepticism becomes gloriously explicit at the moment when the artful Duke is stymied by the stubborn refusal of the atheistical and philistine Barnardine to die in Claudio's place. "Careless, reckless, and fearless of what's past, present, or to come" (IV. ii. 139–40), Barnardine is indifferent to the injury his defiance inflicts upon the formal beauty of the Duke's project, and indeed he comes close to dissolving the lovely artifice into thin air. "I swear I will not die today for any man's persuasion" (IV. iii. 56–57), Barnardine says as he returns to his cell. As he cuts off the Duke's comic entreaties in mid-sentence with a curt "Not a word" (59), we momentarily experience the limits of the Duke's creative word.

The expedient discovery of a dead pirate, who looks just like Claudio, keeps the Duke's enterprise from collapsing at that point, but Shakespeare seems unable to refrain from flooding the whole ridiculous business with some light mocking commentary. When the Duke meets Pompey, for instance, he cannot refrain from berating him as "a bawd, a wicked bawd!" (III. ii. 17). As he proceeds to lambast the bawd for "The evil that thou causest to be done, / That is thy means to live" (18–19), he uses language that reflects back on his own activities as a procurer of willing females. After all, he has just fifteen lines earlier dispatched Isabella to make surreptitious arrangements for a sexual encounter between Angelo and Mariana. Shakespeare's humorous awareness of the degree of overlap in the activities of the bawd and the Duke-Dramatist is heard in Lucio's comment on Pompey's imprisonment. "What," Lucio says in mock astonishment, "is there none of Pygmalion's images newly made woman to be had now, for putting the hand in the pocket and extracting it clutched?" (III. ii. 42–45). The fanciful allusion is to Pompey's present inability easily to procure whores for those with available pocket money, but the curious reference to "Pygmalion's images" may also remind us of the massive intrusion of transforming art the Duke has recently introduced into the play. The Duke is himself a kind of Pygmalion, Shakespeare suggests, in that he too seems able to create from nothing such a "newly made woman" as Mariana to serve his purposes in a sexual role. Although the Duke's art is working its metamorphoses in Vienna it is running into great resistance from an intransigent human nature and is accompanied with an ironic commentary by Shakespeare.

Our last example suggests that the most recalcitrant piece of human nature the Duke has to contend with, after Barnardine, is Lucio's irrepressible tongue. It seems as if the shadow and silence that descends on Isabella, Angelo, and Claudio after the Duke's appearance has only increased the volume of Lucio's irresponsible and slanderous discourse. All the linguistic vitality of the play's first half has been channeled into that prolix mouthpiece, and it is a mistake to regard him simply as a comic foil for the Duke. His running criticisms of the Duke do occasionally hit their mark,[30] but it is the sheer fantastic inventiveness of his elaborate metaphors (as in the example above) that actually does more injury to the prosaic and colorless Duke than his playful slanders, which the Duke takes far too seriously. The Duke's penchant for secrecy takes on an odd coloring when Lucio describes him as "the old fantastical Duke of dark corners" (IV. iii. 154–55), and Lucio's constant exaggerations of the Duke's suppressed creaturality partially undercut his drive towards a cold dispassionate control of events. "The Duke,"

[30] The subtle impact of Lucio's encounters with the Duke are fully and intelligently set forth by Weil, pp. 61–64. See also his more recent essay, "The Options of the Audience: Theory and Practice in Peter Brooks' 'Measure for Measure,'" *Shakespeare Survey*, 25 (1972), 27–35. Weil's essays are quite helpful in stressing the comic tonality of the play, but he tends to overlook its more somber and tragic elements in an effort to make his point. Josephine W. Bennett does even greater violence to the complexities of *Measure* in this regard in *"Measure for Measure" as Royal Entertainment* (New York: Columbia Univ. Press, 1966), when she concludes that "the play is, from beginning to end, pure comedy, based on absurdity, like *The Mikado*" (p. 158).

Lucio tells the supposed Friar, "would eat mutton on Fridays. . . . he would mouth with a beggar, though she smelt brown bread and garlic" (III. ii. 169–72). Lucio's bawdy talk constantly interrupts the smooth symmetry of the Act V theatricals, despite the Duke's exasperated demands to "Silence that fellow" (V. i. 181). And we joy in his presence because he stands alone as a piece of embarrassing reality that cannot be subsumed into a formal artifact by the Duke's powerful alchemy. "I am a kind of burr; I shall stick" (IV. iii. 174) he informs the hassled Duke as he accompanies him from the stage in Act IV, and he does.

Lucio finally gets his long delayed comeuppance, of course, but not until the play is a mere fifteen lines away from its ending, and so not before he has done noticeable damage to the ostensible solemnity of the play's climax. "You were not bid to speak," the Duke warns him as the final action gets under way, but Lucio's snappy reply—"No, my good lord, / Nor wished to hold my peace" (V. i. 78–79)—asserts his single independence from the Duke's plot. Thus, the dense richness of his language contributes to Shakespeare's critique of Duke Vincentio's actions by reminding us of that verbal medium the Duke has had to suppress in his attempt to reassert human control through the agency of a teleological action. The Duke's frustrated efforts to muzzle Lucio reveal Shakespeare's awareness that a basic inadequacy, or one-sidedness, exists in his whole mode of operation: a misuse of the full resources of poetic drama. As in *Romeo and Juliet* and *Troilus and Cressida,* neither language nor action is ultimately adequate as a medium to respond to the problems raised in the play. In fact, those two components of poetic drama appear to work against each other with no real possibility of reconciliation. Unlike the former plays, however, Shakespeare is now unwilling to push that dual inadequacy in his medium to its logical conclusion. Instead, he allows Vincentio his grand formal triumph in Act V, even though he himself seems unable fully to endorse the Duke's simplified formula for artistic success. A poetic that guarantees victory by advancing the consolations of formal control at the expense of linguistic vitality is not a solution consistent with Shakespeare's finer dramatic achievements.

V

The highly self-conscious organization of Vincentio's return to power—the elaborate formality of the controlled movements and utterances of the participants—can affect us only in a contained and detached way. Vincentio plays out his masquerade with great flair, but his actions lack the dramatic energy to reach out and engage the audience. Instead, his drama must be content to rotate smoothly within the small orbit of its own self-enclosed and programmed mechanism. We feel increasingly distanced from any meaningful response as it becomes clear that the Duke is performing his miraculous discoveries not for us but for the small, very appreciative audience of people on stage: characters who are abjectly vulnerable to his protracted revelations of omniscience. Thus, the entire last act seems to exist on a level of performance and significance mostly tangential to the main body of the play. As Mincoff succinctly puts it, "We are left to get excited if we can over tensions that do not exist, and over the conflicting testimonies of an imbroglio in which no one is embroiled." [31] A disorienting gap opens between the simple emotional responses elicited by the various peripeteias, which the now all-powerful Duke forces upon the helpless characters, and the logical and thematic expectations aroused earlier by the general complexity of the play. The subtle dialectics between nature and art and speech and action are simply absorbed into the manifest, indivisible authority of Duke Vincentio, under whose omnipotent guidance the play recedes quickly into the realm of artifice and make-believe. To suppose the Duke's great show of power somehow arbitrates those difficult issues is to substitute for Shakespeare's play one more congenial to critical synthesis.

The various parts that make up *Measure for Measure* do not finally come together to form a satisfactorily unified structure or vision. Despite the constant recourse to strategies of specious mediation, the play concludes, as it began, on a strong note of disjunction. Shakespeare's awareness of the way in which his play has failed to achieve a convincing mediation of its extremes can be felt in the rather half-hearted effort he makes to convince us of the marriage between Vincentio and Isabella.[32] During the deceptions and discoveries that crowd the play's ending, the Duke finds time to make two separate, unrelated proposals to the would-be Nun that are as awkward examples of courtship as Shakespeare ever wrote. As he makes the supposedly executed Claudio suddenly materialize before Isabella, he abruptly breaks the

---

[31] Mincoff, p. 149.

[32] I cannot agree with Weil's assertion in "Form and Contexts" that "the wedding of Misogynist Duke-Friar to the chaste novice Isabella, who 'most abhors' the sexual vice of her brother, achieves a comic rightness" (p. 67). Weil does point out here the ludicrous nature of the misalliance, but he tends to dissolve those differences in an overall comic ambience I find hard to accept. There is a "rightness" about the tentative marriage, but it is not "comic."

spell of the reunion by saying bluntly, "Give me your hand and say you will be mine" (V. i. 488). Isabella makes no response, either to her brother or to the Duke. Again, just as the play concludes, the Duke terminates his self-congratulating summary of final character dispositions with another offer.

> Dear Isabel,
> I have a motion much imports your good,
> Whereto if you'll a willing ear incline,
> What's mine is yours, and what is yours is mine.
> (V. i. 529–32)

Once again Isabella stands silent as the play appropriately ends with the whole issue of a possible reconciliation of differences in a symbolic, comic marriage left precariously suspended on the thread of that hypothetical "if." The possibility of marriage is even further attenuated by the diminished response expected of Isabella, who is not to speak her acceptance but passively "a willing ear incline" to his active gesture. The two characters tentatively face each other as the play ends, forming a suggestive emblem of the whole, for they visually express both Shakespeare's desire for a valid harmonization of opposites and his recognition here of unbridgeable differences. Isabella's powerfully expressive silence reminds us how much the play itself has been a curious misalliance of the abstract and concrete, the tongue and heart, the theoretical and erotic, the artificial and natural. The awkwardness of the two proposals recalls other awkward moments of forced mediation—such as the handy availability of Mariana or the ludicrous substitution of Ragozine's head—and reminds us how much the comic solution depends upon patterns of fraudulent mediation. As a play celebrating the harmonizing powers of poetic drama, *Measure for Measure* does not succeed. As another instance in Shakespeare's ongoing exploration into the contradictory tendencies in both life and art, however, it achieves a disturbingly masterful articulation.

IV BEYOND EXTREMITY:

King Lear and the Limits of Poetic Drama

❧

> *This would have seemed a period*
> *To such as love not sorrow; but another,*
> *To amplify too much, would make much more,*
> *And top extremity.*
> (V. iii. 205–08)

Unlike *Troilus and Cressida* and *Measure for Measure, King Lear* has not had to endure the indignity of prolonged neglect. Nor is there any indication in the recent flurry of critical and theatrical activity that its present glory is beginning to wane. Yet we seem able to acknowledge the play's high eminence and still admit to nagging doubts and irritating cavils concerning its overall coherence as a work of dramatic art. However superlative, our praise seems almost inadvertently to bring forth embarrassing qualifications. These reservations about *King Lear's* perfection spring in large part from an uneasy feeling that Shakespeare, either out of naiveté or dramatic misjudgment, succumbs in the play to that "artistic greediness" T. S. Eliot identified as the prime cause of Renaissance drama's "unwillingness to accept any limitation and abide by it." [1] Shakespeare appears to share with his overweening protagonist an impatience with the constraints of medium. For just as King Lear rashly banishes the limiting mediacy exemplified by Cordelia and Kent, Shakespeare seems determined to circumvent the demeaning necessity of confining his vision within the prescribed agencies of language and staged action. [2] The impression arises that the playwright may be over-

[1] T. S. Eliot, *Selected Essays* (New York: Harcourt, Brace and World, 1932), p. 98.
[2] Sigurd Burckhardt, in a brilliant essay entitled *"King Lear:* The Quality of Nothing," calls attention to a basic dynamic involving the concepts of mediacy

reaching on the same heroic scale as is his impetuous old king, since both men subject their respective kingdoms to unrealizable demands.

Shakespeare's willingness to violate dramatic decorum in *King Lear* has generated some sharp protest. Coleridge qualified his appreciation of the play, for instance, with the complaint that Shakespeare went too far when he staged Gloucester's blinding. "I will not disguise my conviction, that in this one point the tragic in the play has been urged beyond the outermost mark and *ne plus ultra* of the dramatic."[3] Dr. Johnson had previously found "the extrusion of Gloucester's eyes . . . an act too horrid to be endured in dramatic exhibition," but he felt that the play reached its true *ne plus ultra* in the shocking spectacle of the strangled Cordelia in Lear's arms.[4] Still, the dramatic impropriety of the play is not always condemned. Herman Melville saw those occasions when Shakespeare seemed to urge the action beyond the limits of formal representation not as moments of lamentable misjudgment so much as transcendent instances of visionary breakthrough: occasions when Truth frees itself from the specious mediacy of dramatic convention and speaks with an oracular immediacy. Melville located such radiant moments not in Gloucester's gory blinding nor in the breathtaking exposure of a hanged daughter's body but rather in the excoriating mad speeches in which "tormented into desperation, Lear, the frantic king, tears off the mask, and speaks the sane madness of vital truth."[5] In their own characteristic ways Johnson, Coleridge, and Melville isolated particularly striking instances of what we now recognize in *King Lear* as a general tendency to explore states of experience seemingly beyond extremity. They remind us that Shakespeare's unique achievement in this play goes hand in hand with a compulsive urge to extend the boundaries of his medium "beyond the outermost mark" of the dramatic—and that the achievement should be understood in the context of a compulsion.

King Lear's sprawling, overflowing quality—its refusal to rest content within its spacious formal dimensions—leaves it open, then, to

---

and immediacy in *King Lear*. I found this original essay very stimulating. See his book *Shakespearean Meanings* (Princeton: Princeton Univ. Press, 1968). The *King Lear* essay is on pp. 237–59.

[3] S. T. Coleridge, *Shakespearean Criticism,* ed. T. M. Raysor (New York: Dutton, 1960), vol. I, p. 51.

[4] Samuel Johnson, *Johnson on Shakespeare,* ed. Walter Raleigh (London: Oxford Univ. Press, 1952), pp. 159–60.

[5] Herman Melville, "Hawthorne and His Mosses" (1850), reprinted in *The Shock of Recognition,* ed. Edmund Wilson (New York: Grosset and Dunlap, 1943), pp. 187–204. The remark quoted is on p. 193.

objection from those who accept Eliot's classical *dictum* that "a work of art should be self-consistent" and that "an artist should consciously draw a circle beyond which he does not trespass." [6] Indeed, modern commentators have charged that Shakespeare's appetite for extreme situations has driven him for once into areas of experience that simply cannot be contained within the limited scope of the stage or even within the more broadly conceived parameters of poetic drama. For instance, J. Middleton Murry believes that Shakespeare momentarily lost sight of the inherent capacities of his medium and thus "did not master his material." Because "it is lacking in imaginative control," Murry classifies *King Lear* with *Troilus, Measure,* and *Timon*: plays in which formal articulation capitulates to an obscure obsessive intent. [7] W. C. B. Watkins more generously notes that the play "is unquestionably Shakespeare's most nearly all-inclusive tragedy," and that "Shakespeare is working on a grander scale than before or after"; yet he too feels constrained to show how *"King Lear* attempts too much." [8] The same critical ambivalence informs Philip Edwards' recent judgment that *King Lear* "is certainly his most ambitious play," but that "in its huge orchestration, it is always threatening to go beyond the powers of any stage or any actor —Elizabethan or otherwise." [9] Such discomfiture arises not merely from the magnitude, complexity, and overcrowding of the action, although such overloading is often viewed as a structural flaw. Rather, that school of criticism glimpses in the play a more fundamental misunderstanding of the basic capacities of the genre. Margaret Webster asserts that *King Lear* always fails on the stage because "the capacities of actors and audience alike . . . are strained beyond the limits of the theater medium." [10] Webster voices her charge of formal superfluity, we should note, in phrases that echo Coleridge's protest over the play's excessive cruelty. In fact, it is quite remarkable how indispensable that "beyond" locution ("go beyond," "urged beyond," "trespass beyond," "strained beyond," etc.) apparently is to the criticism of *King Lear.* Whether our attention is directed to the play's substance (by Johnson and Coleridge) or fixed on the play's structure (by Edwards and Webster) we seem inevitably

[6] Eliot, p. 93.

[7] J. Middleton Murry, *Shakespeare* (London: Jonathan Cape, 1936), p. 284.

[8] W. C. B. Watkins, *Shakespeare and Spenser* (Princeton: Princeton Univ. Press, 1950), p. 107.

[9] Philip Edwards, *Shakespeare and the Confines of Art* (London: Methuen, 1968), p. 128.

[10] Margaret Webster, *Shakespeare Today* (London: J. M. Dent & Sons, 1957), p. 220.

to encounter an artist intent on exploding customary systems of coherence and frames of representation.

By briefly surveying these several expressions of discontent with Shakespeare's artistry, it becomes possible to gain a less negative point of view concerning the play's formal and thematic peculiarities. Not only the long-suffering Lear but also the capacities of actors, audience, and stage—along with the formal resources of plot and scenario, language and characterization—seem unnaturally overburdened by the creative impulse behind the play. The very pervasiveness of the effects of that impulse suggests an unusual form of coherence. It may be that Shakespeare's general insistence on straining the faculties "beyond the outermost mark and *ne plus ultra*" directs us to the formative action (or *praxis*) that unifies and reveals the full imaginative design of the play.[11] Edgar perhaps describes that action most succinctly in the phrase "to top extremity," which he uses during a sequence of rapidly accelerating sorrows in Act V. Around that generative idea all the poetic and dramatic components of *King Lear* cohere into a whole of unparalleled power. Shakespeare's experimentation with his medium has taken him to the point where he can create the effect of going beyond extremity in regard to theme and structure while nevertheless working confidently, as Eliot would wish, within the expanded circle of his craft. By appearing to violate dramatic propriety, while actually endowing his art with new force and magnitude, he can exploit his medium to create a desired illusion of immediacy. In the light of this unique and paradoxical poetic, most of the misgivings about excessiveness, lack of mastery over materials, and undisciplined greediness should evaporate in the face of an achieved dramatic purpose. Moreover, *King Lear* should emerge as the one play examined in this book where Shakespeare's medium proves fully responsive to his vision of a tragic human insufficiency. We will first consider plot and scenario, then turn to an examination of language and character.

I

King Lear's plot unfolds scenically by repeatedly moving its participants to stages of suffering, which seem to have reached the ultimate degree of bearable intensity, only to open before their startled eyes even more distressing vistas of anguish and humiliation. Consequently,

[11] I am using the Aristotelian concept of *praxis* in the sense that Francis Fergusson explains and employs it in *The Idea of a Theater: The Art of Drama in Changing Perspective* (Princeton: Princeton Univ. Press, 1949).

an implicit colloquy gradually develops between various characters and the onrushing events, in which the oppressed can be heard to say what the dying Edmund says to his half brother Edgar: "but speak you on—/ You look as you had something more to say" (V. iii. 201–02). Edmund's premonition of "something more" is especially disturbing in this particular instance, since it is said in response to Edgar's agonized recital of an incident of recent double extremity in which his father's "flawed heart —/ Alack, too weak the conflict to support—/ 'Twixt two extremes of passion, joy and grief, / Burst smilingly" (197–200). Ignoring Albany's plea—"If there be more, more woeful, hold it in"—Edgar responds to Edmund's request by passing beyond his father's death to tell of another incident of grief, which he says will top the extremity of all former disasters.

> This would have seemed a period
> To such as love not sorrow; but another,
> To amplify too much, would make much more,
> And top extremity.
> (V. iii. 205–08)

Edgar then tells of Kent's sudden appearance and of his "most piteous tale of Lear and him / That ever ear received" (215–16)—a tale, Edgar says, which so affects Kent that he suffers a cracking of "the strings of life" (217). It is paradigmatic of the action imitated in *King Lear* that even this brief series of instances of ultra-extreme suffering is again abruptly and immeasurably topped, first by the unexpected display of the self-slaughtered sisters Goneril and Regan and then by the jarring eruption into the darkening scene of the ruined king himself with his dead daughter in his arms.[12] Faced with this penultimate epiphany of utterly gratuitous death, Albany can reasonably dismiss the previous misfortunes—terrible enough at the time—as "but a trifle here." "Here" is a suitably inadequate euphemism for the dark unspeakable space of Lear's inconsolable grief for his lost daughter. By propelling us from one extremity to another in this manner, Shakespeare forces us finally to acquiesce in the knowledge that *King Lear* will offer no condition this side of the grave that can be accepted as terminal.

That series of interlocking events illustrates how Shakespeare focuses attention on the inexorable disintegration of a complex and manifold universe. *King Lear*'s world is in a dynamic state of irrever-

[12] See the perceptive discussion of the Lear-Job "o'ertopping extremity" theme in John Holloway, *The Story of the Night: Studies in Shakespeare's Major Tragedies* (London: Kegan Paul, 1961), pp. 85–98.

sible decomposition, and the degree to which Shakespeare is able to orchestrate and sustain his sense of an ordered world's collapse testifies to the visionary power behind the conception. That collapse can appear sudden and precipitous as in Gloucester's mutilation and fall from Edgar's Dover Cliff, but more often it will assume a gradual, articulated pattern like that of Lear's protracted humiliations. As Lear declines to "an O without a figure" (I. iv. 183), Shakespeare symbolizes the deterioration of his majesty through the analogous action of Goneril's and Regan's prolonged reduction of his one hundred knights. They chip away at the initial unity of "100," dividing it into ever-diminishing quantities of "50," "25," "10," "5," "1," until eventually nothing remains either of his former dignity or of his royal retinue of knights. We also experience the world's disintegration in the progression of events from spacious castle to heath to beggarly hovel; in the worsening of weather conditions from fair to cataclysmic storm; in the change of pacing and rhythm in stage movements from graceful ritual and stately ceremony to the spastic convulsions of devil-tormented madmen; in the modulation of utterance from the solemn pronouncements of royal prerogative to the screams and fragmented ejaculations of disoriented minds; in the dramatically effective change in attire from princely gorgeousness to dirty rags and nakedness; and in many other patterns of radical reversal by now well known to students of the play.[13] In all cases, the progressions suggest a compulsion to press beyond extremity by stripping away all that mediates between man and a direct encounter with his universe.

When near the middle of the play Gloucester advises Kent to "take him in thy arms. . . . Take up thy master" (III. iv. 86–90), we should perceive how the action has gradually driven "Royal Lear" from his original state of total freedom of motion into a more and more restricted range of movement and influence. The self-deposed king wanders from his castle to his nobles' smaller homes—"This house is little" (II. iv. 283), Regan says of Gloucester's place—from the crowded hovel to his sickbed, and then to the childlike enclosure of Kent's arms. As the play continues to press beyond extremity, we see Lear on his litter, in a chair from which he staggers to kneel abjectly at Cordelia's feet, on his way to a prison, which he imagines as a birdcage, and finally, staring with catatonic intensity upon Cordelia's motionless face

[13] For example, see Holloway, pp. 81–84; Thomas McFarland, *Tragic Meanings in Shakespeare* (New York: Random House, 1966), pp. 153–56; William R. Elton, *"King Lear" and the Gods* (San Marino, Calif.: The Huntington Library, 1966), pp. 329–34.

while he struggles against his own imminent death. By means of such a brilliantly variegated chain of verbal and visual images, Shakespeare exploits the resources of his medium in order to depict the gradual removal of space and freedom from Lear. The autocratic monarch who would abolish all between-ness—"Come not between the dragon and his wrath"—now experiences a constricting immediacy. For in the last moments of his life we realize that all his former world—"With shadowy forests and with champains riched, / With plenteous rivers and wide-skirted meads" (I. i. 64–65)—as Granville-Barker observes, "has narrowed to the dead Cordelia in his arms."[14] Such a detailed imaging of the shrinkage of Lear's scope gives to the old king's pilgrimage into extremity the faint suggestion of something approaching demonic revelation: a *katagogic* progression that reaches its nadir when Lear is forced to gaze with heart-stopping horror on the still lips of his murdered child.

As those illustrations suggest, Shakespeare delineates in *King Lear* the full variety of the observable human scene, but he so arranges the plentitude that it seems always to be giving way before an imminent nothingness. This peculiar technique is perhaps most noticeable in Edgar's astonishing evocation of the imagined view from Dover Cliff. He convinces his mutilated and despairing father that he has positioned him on the "extreme verge" of that "cliff, whose high and bending head / Looks fearfully in the confinèd deep" (IV. i. 73–74). Although Edgar exclaims "How fearful / And dizzy 'tis to cast one's eyes so low!" he nevertheless proceeds calmly and minutely to describe the plunging perspective supposedly before them.[15]

> The crows and choughs that wing the midway air
> Show scarce so gross as beetles. Halfway down
> Hangs one that gathers sampire—dreadful trade;
> Methinks he seems no bigger than his head.

[14] Harley Granville-Barker, *Prefaces to Shakespeare* (Princeton: Princeton Univ. Press, 1947) vol. 1, p. 300.

[15] In the analysis that follows I have been aided by Marshall McLuhan's remarks on Edgar's speech in his *The Gutenberg Galaxy: The Making of Typographic Man* (Toronto: Univ. of Toronto Press, 1962), pp. 11–19, and in his more recent book, *Through the Vanishing Point: Space in Poetry and Painting* (New York: Harper and Row, 1968), pp. 74–75. Also very useful to me was Harry Levin's "The Heights and the Depths: A Scene from *King Lear*," in *More Talking of Shakespeare,* ed. John Garrett (London: Longmans, Green, 1959), and Alvin B. Kernan's, "Formalism and Realism in Elizabethan Drama: The Miracles in *King Lear*," *Renaissance Drama,* 9 (1966), 59–66.

> The fishermen that walk upon the beach
> Appear like mice; and yond tall anchoring bark,
> Diminished to her cock; her cock, a buoy
> Almost too small for sight. The murmuring surge
> That on th' unnumb'red idle pebble chafes
> Cannot be heard so high. I'll look no more, . . .
> (IV. vi. 11–22)

The view's static serenity oddly belies the dramatic urgency of Gloucester's plight. The sharp clarity of the vision—the sense of precisely observed and carefully distanced physical detail—results largely from the
fact that it is composed of several planes that diminish in rigidly controlled perspective to the vanishing point of the buoy / Almost too
small for sight." In fact, we should recognize here a formal principle
similar to the numerical reduction of Lear's knights, who also undergo
distinctly marked stages of diminishment before they too vanish into
nothingness. Edgar's words create a structural perspective in which
crows shrink to beetles and fishermen look like mice, that subtly recalls
the general progressions of symphonic diminution outlined above. Indeed, this sophisticated use of visual planes seems designed to remind us
of the play's interest in the rich density of ordinary existence and, con-
versely, of its essential instability. The central figure of the dangling
sampire-gatherer is a striking image of the precarious between-ness of
the human condition: his "dreadful trade" perhaps recalling the vul-
nerability of such mediators as Cordelia and Kent, who futilely attempt
to stand between Lear and the abyss that awaits him. Under Edgar's
control our gaze sweeps downward through the mediacy of sampire-
gatherer, fishermen, beach, bark, and buoy, until we reach the shapeless
expanse of sea beyond that outermost mark. Lear himself is following
a similar trajectory.

Edgar warns of the fearful consequences of "cast[ing] one's
eyes so low," and at the moment his eye reaches the limits of vision he
suddenly breaks off, exclaiming,

> I'll look no more,
> Lest my brain turn, and the deficient sight
> Topple down headlong.
> (IV. vi. 22–24)

The vertigo Edgar imagines himself experiencing results not from the
contemplation of the diminishing planes so much as from the awareness
that he is being carried beyond the range of the eyes' structuring faculty:

beyond the range of the senses in general. By acknowledging that unstructured area of "deficient sight," Edgar becomes sensitive to other qualities in the overall picture definable only by negation.[16] The "murmuring surge" of the sea, for instance, "cannot be heard" from the summit, and the "idle pebble[s]" on the beach are "unnumb'red." After his imagined fall from the cliff Edgar tells Gloucester that "Ten masts at each make not the altitude / Which thou hast perpendicularly fell" (53–54). Just as the sea could not be heard from the top, now from the base "The shrill-gorged lark so far / Cannot be seen or heard" (58–59). The entire episode, despite its fine evocation of graphic particularity, demonstrates a general inadequacy of apprehension. Hence Edgar remarks, "your other senses grow imperfect / By your eyes' anguish" (5–6). We never forget that the entirety of Edgar's speech is finally an artful structuring of nothing because a felt absence permeates the whole elaborate deception. Edgar's fertile imagination forms a reality that temporarily saves his father from suicidal despair, but a strong undercurrent of radical denial weakens the thrust of his effort. Edgar himself aptly calls it a "trifle" (33), and Shakespeare quickly shatters the fragile artifact by suddenly introducing into the scene the mad weed-bedecked king with his unstructured mixture of "matter and impertinency" (171).[17]

    This climactic episode repeatedly reminds us that Shakespeare's concern is with the exploration of areas of experience seemingly beyond the range of mental, visual, and linguistic articulation. The suggestion in Edgar's speech of qualities beyond the capacities of the senses may recall A. C. Bradley's intuition that "there is something in *King Lear*'s very essence which is at war with the senses," something that "not only refuses to reveal itself fully through the senses but seems to be almost in contradiction with their report."[18] Bradley implies that the representation of this essence is impossible because of the inherent limitations of the dramatic medium and that the play is flawed by the grandeur of its own conception. Edgar's lines show, however, that Shakespeare has learned to deploy the resources of poetic language and stage so as to produce sudden moments of illumination that function dramatically to give body and dimension to a circumambient darkness. He can flood our minds with an awareness of that formless essence by

[16] A similar observation is made by Levin in his essay on Edgar's speech.

[17] See Burckhardt's illuminating analysis of the effect of Lear's mad speeches on the Gloucester-Edgar experience, pp. 248–54.

[18] A. C. Bradley, *Shakespearean Tragedy: Lectures on "Hamlet," "Othello," "King Lear," "Macbeth"* (London: Macmillan, 1904, reprint 1967), p. 247.

gradually bringing us to the extreme point where the senses capitulate to a knowledge beyond their scope. Thus, at climactic moments in the play characters experience violent juxtapositions of darkness and revelation. For instance, Gloucester's blinding is followed immediately by his realization of Edgar's innocence. Having reached the dark nadir of his physical suffering he achieves the full revelation of his past ignorance: "O my follies! Then Edgar was abused" (III. vii. 91).[19] A quite similar moment occurs at the play's ending when Kent chants "All's cheerless, dark, and deadly" (V. iii. 291) as the dying king studies the face of his dead child and catches glimpses of the truth that "She's dead as earth." The primary effect of those flashes of revelation is to give substance and meaning to the darkness out of which they arise; just as the mute tableau of Lear's and Cordelia's bodies at the conclusion throws into almost epiphanic clarity the nature of their experience.

In the generally deteriorating world of *King Lear* neither Edgar's well-intentioned fictions nor Shakespeare's customary artistry can finally contain the phenomenon unfolding dynamically before them; their contrived systems point beyond their demonstrated limitations. In fact, the play reveals a deep distrust of all attempts at closure. Only Edmund can say "The wheel is come full circle; I am here" (V. iii. 175), for his dying vision of a patterned, end-stopped life cycle is the ironic reward of a career devoid of real contact with humanity. Such a closed and symmetrical existence is not available to those characters capable of sympathetic participation in life. "Let go thy hold when a great wheel runs down a hill," the Fool advises Kent, "lest it break thy neck with following" (II. iv. 68–70). Those unable to heed this warning find themselves caught up in a gathering momentum that sweeps them over precipices into uncharted areas of depravation and grief. For instance, Edgar may feel confident that, as Poor Tom o' Bedlam, he has reached the extremity of his adversity and that he is at a point on the Wheel of Fortune where "The worst returns to laughter" (IV. i. 6). But this venerable trope, proper for his bastard brother, is immediately discredited by his encounter with his badly maimed father and his subsequent recognition that their interrelated fates are evolving in an open universe where there is no "worst." Sitting in Cornwall's stocks, Kent consoles himself by invoking Fortune to

<hr>

[19] For a fine discussion of this aspect of the play and an excellent general study of *King Lear* see Stanley Cavell's *Must We Mean What We Say? Modern Philosophical Essays in Morality, Religion, Drama, Music, and Criticism* (New York: Scribner's, 1969). See the chapter entitled, "The Avoidance of Love: A Reading of *King Lear*," pp. 267–353.

"Smile once more; turn thy wheel" (II. ii. 169), but he too is never to experience a "return to laughter." Like Gloucester stepping from "the extreme verge" of Dover Cliff into the imagined void, the play urges the action beyond all forms of containment. Standing "on the very verge / Of [Nature's] confine" (II. iv. 142–43), Lear is stripped of his knights, reduced to pathetic displays of rage and self-pity, degraded to the extreme state of "unaccommodated man," and then, when release seems possible, precipitated into a madness that threatens to become—like Poor Tom's "lake of darkness"—unfathomable. Cordelia and Edgar not only suffer excommunication and banishment but are forced beyond that extremity into an ontological condition expressible only negatively as nothing.[20] Bottomless experiences await them because, unlike Edmund, they are related essentially to each other. Their descent has no perceivable terminus, no promised end.

II

To become conscious of the peculiarly open-ended nature of *King Lear*'s plot movement allows us to understand better the significance of several isolated moments of optimism and sudden resurgence of hope. It seems clear, as we follow the play's progression, that such hope is repeatedly aroused primarily to create occasions to plunge both characters and audience into darker areas of despair. In fact, much good recent criticism of *King Lear* has concerned itself with mapping the precise maneuvers involved in Shakespeare's campaign against cosmic and terrestrial optimism.[21] V. A. Kolve, for example, recognizes that the temporary movement towards happiness and recognition in the Act IV reunion between Lear and Cordelia turns out to be "only a way of revitalizing that suffering, of restoring feeling to nerves nearly deadened with pain." [22] The stronger upsurge of optimism,

[20] See Holloway's remarks on this general "descent into chaos," pp. 76–84.

[21] Holloway: "Repeatedly, we are made to think that since Nature is an order (though doubtless a stern one) release from suffering is at hand; but instead, the suffering is renewed. . . . The bitter reversal of events comes again and again" pp. 88–89). Elton, Chapter 11, "Irony as Structure," pp. 329–34. Nicholas Brooke, *"King Lear,"* Studies in English Literature, no. 15 (London: Edward Arnold, 1963), lays a heavy stress on the play's continual repudiation of comforting ideas in the last two Acts. "The last two Acts of the play," Brooke says, "are constructed of a series of advances and repudiations of visions of hope. Each concept is followed by a scene of intense experience to which the idea cannot be applied" (p. 58).

[22] V. A. Kolve, "The Modernity of *Lear,"* *Pacific Coast Studies in Shakespeare,* ed. Waldo F. McNeir and Thelma N. Greenfield (Eugene, Ore.: Univ. of Oregon Press, 1966), p. 185.

generated by Edgar's chivalric and triumphant reentrance into the action in the Act V duel, has a similar purpose, since even more emphatic action is now required to awaken any hope in us for Lear and Cordelia after their abrupt defeat and imprisonment. But this hope is again brutally frustrated and mocked by the ensuing action. As in Edgar's Dover Cliff speech, the levels of hope arrest us only momentarily before dropping all concerned still closer to the all-engulfing sea.

    King Lear's cruel progression towards unrelieved despair is not an insight of modern critics alone. Nahum Tate, the seventeenth-century dramatist, was apparently, and understandably, shocked by the bleakness of the play's vision of life and set himself the task of correcting Shakespeare's impiety in his infamous redaction (first produced in 1681). Although he does mostly succeed in eradicating the play's disturbing nihilism, he leaves a curious remnant of Shakespeare's "darker purpose," which catches perfectly the peculiar quality we have been examining. At the conclusion of Tate's play, Edgar and Albany rush into the prison to rescue Lear and Cordelia from their murderers. Having assured their safety, Albany pronounces the happy resolution of Lear's prolonged misfortunes.

> Take off their Chains—Thou injur'd Majesty,
> The Wheel of Fortune now hath made her Circle,
> And Blessings yet stand 'twixt thy Grave and thee.
> (V. vi. 61–63)[23]

Still fixed in momentary despair, Lear responds to Albany's promising words with a deep bitterness that takes us back to the demonic experience of Shakespeare's eclipsed play rather than to Tate's tamed revision.

> Com'st thou, inhuman Lord, to sooth us back
> To a Fool's Paradise of Hope, to make
> Our Doom more wretched? Go to, we are too well
> Acquainted with Misfortune, to be gulled
> With lying hope; no, we will hope no more.
> (V. vi. 64–68)

Tate's miserable redaction is itself a "Fool's Paradise of Hope," but

[23] For Nahum Tate's redaction of *King Lear* together with his important dedicatory letter explaining his intentions, see *Five Restoration Adaptations of Shakespeare,* ed. Christopher Spencer (Urbana, Ill.: Univ. of Illinois Press, 1965), pp. 203–74.

there is little doubt that he did perfectly well know just how horrible
the experience of Shakespeare's play could be when faced unflinchingly.
That he, along with Dr. Johnson and two centuries of stage history,
did not choose to face it directly testifies to the power of its vision.

The old king, whom even Tate is unable to defeat, has experienced the gradual erosion of all trust in delusive hope, the disillusionment of faith in human and divine justice, and, finally, the loss
of even the simple will to live. In Shakespeare's play that condition
has been brought about by the gradual cumulation of reversals of hope,
which eventually broaden to include the clashing ironies of the last act.
Shakespeare controls those ironies with amazing virtuosity. Even
though we are aware rather early in the play of our participation in
the recurrent pattern of hope and despair, we respond yet once again
with dismay when Albany's pious wish that "The gods defend her!"
(V. iii. 257) is instantly answered by the jolting appearance of the
enraged old king carrying his hanged daughter. The gradual intensi-
fying of ironic reversals operates, William R. Elton says, "like a series
of trap-doors," [24] plunging us down a little further each time until
we finally begin to intuit despair and perhaps even begin to catch
glimpses of that "demonic grin" G. W. Knight discerned at the heart
of *King Lear*.[25] The lines that Tate permitted his exhausted old king
to utter capture perfectly the state of mind in which the final scene
leaves the audience and the surviving characters: "Go to, we are too
well / Acquainted with Misfortune, to be gulled / With lying hope;
no, we will hope no more." The play's scenario has been carefully designed "to sooth us back / To a Fool's Paradise of Hope" in order,
finally, to make "Our Doom more wretched." Such heightening of
extreme suffering by raising and exploiting false hopes may remind
us of Aaron the Moor's diabolical toying with Titus, and indeed the
contrast between *Titus Andronicus* and *Lear* should help us better
understand Shakespeare's handling of characterization in *Lear*. But
first we should inquire more precisely into the ways that language
participates in the basic action of the play.

III

In no play does Shakespeare make more brilliant use of the
full resources of language to reveal complex and dynamic personality

[24] Elton, p. 330.
[25] G. W. Knight, *The Wheel of Fire: Interpretations of Shakespearian Tragedy*
(London: Methuen, 1930, reprinted, 1949), p. 175.

than in *King Lear*. A single of Lear's speeches gives, as Edwards notes, "the very fluctuations and contradictions that make personality." [26] Language is usually adequate to express the extremity of experience in *Lear*; yet the play's persistent urge to "top" that extremity tremendously strains even a fully responsive linguistic medium. Shakespeare seems determined, especially in the middle section of the play, to pit language against the most extreme instances of hostile nature and circumstance. Lear threatens to "outscorn / The to-and-fro-conflicting wind and rain" (III. i. 10–11), and Edgar vows to "outface / The winds and persecutions of the sky" (II. iii. 11–12). Even the Fool participates in this verbal duel with adversity, since his essential dramatic function seems only to "labor to outjest / [Lear's] heart-struck injuries" (III. i. 16–17). [27] The use of language to defiantly "outface," "outscorn," and "outjest" soul-crushing experiences is clearly an important humanistic weapon in the play's defense against an encroaching darkness. However, Shakespeare's major linguistic effort seems more often directed towards a radically different effect: the exploitation of language to illustrate the final inadequacy of the word-medium, when it is confronted by certain kinds of experiences beyond extremity. [28] Thus, the grand defiance of Lear's magniloquent "Blow winds, and crack your cheeks. Rage, blow" (III. ii. 1) gradually gives way to the verbal collapse of "Thou'lt come no more, / Never, never, never, never, never" (V. iii. 308–09). When brought face to face with an inconceivable horror, the characters have to abandon the "out-doing" *topos* and fall back upon the simplest units of expression, causing bare and humble words to be suddenly charged with miraculously expressive power. As Albany contemplates the unspeakable ingratitude of Goneril to her father, for instance, he concludes that, unless retribution is swift, "It will come" (IV. ii. 48). He lets the colorless pronoun "it" stand euphemistically for a bestial anarchy beyond articulation. Under the increasing pressure of recurrent instances of inexpressible depravity, language in *Lear* strains towards new heights of expression before it finally buckles, surrendering the mode of direct utterance for a more oblique mode of communication.

[26] Edwards, p. 128.
[27] Maynard Mack, *"King Lear" in Our Time* (Berkeley: Univ. of California Press, 1965). There is a good discussion of the importance of this locution on p. 88.
[28] Winifred M. T. Nowottny, "Some Aspects of the Style of *King Lear*," *Shakespeare Survey*, 13 (1960), 49–57, offers an excellent analysis of the play's linguistic peculiarities. This essay has helped me better understand Shakespeare's deployment of language in *King Lear*, as has Paul A. Jorgensen's "A Deed Without a Name," *Pacific Coast Studies in Shakespeare*, ed. Waldo F. McNeir and Thelma N. Greenfield (Eugene, Ore.: Univ. of Oregon Press, 1966), pp. 190–98.

Lear's encounter with Poor Tom in Act III is a good instance of how language functions as an adjunct to vision. The scene climaxes not with the mighty rant and rhetoric heard earlier in the act but with the far more powerful hushed cadence of Lear's "Didst thou give all to thy daughters? And art thou come to this?" (III. iv. 48–49). The stark simplicity of Lear's phrasing, as he identifies with the madman before him and then goes mad himself, creates a quiet sublimity that reminds us again how Shakespeare explores experience apparently beyond the reach of ordinary discourse. Norman Maclean's fine study of the episode has called attention to the astonishing force of the terminal "this" in Lear's question. It jolts us into a recognition that certain moments have a legitimately unmentionable dimension: "spots of experience which, at least in the instantaneous flash of shocked recognition, cannot be fully faced or exactly spoken by those who must endure them." [29] The effect is not unlike that created in Edgar's Dover Cliff speech, where diminishing visual details point beyond themselves to an area unsubjugated by human structures. Lear's final "this" simultaneously calls attention to the capitulation of language in the face of sudden horror and also directs attention to the visual image of that unspeakable horror: "the thing itself," Poor Tom o' Bedlam—the shameful *ne plus ultra* of total human degradation. In a similarly denotative manner, Lear's dying command, "look there, look there" (V. iii. 312), focuses attention simultaneously on both the collapse of language and the speaker, while also pointing to the cause of that collapse: the inarticulate, brute fact of Cordelia's utterly absurd death.

By synchronizing language and stage action in this manner Shakespeare passes beyond the usual confines of his medium into areas of experience so intense as to be expressible only by oblique or even mute suggestion. We have seen a somewhat similar attitude towards the inadequacy of language in *Romeo, Troilus,* and *Measure,* but now Shakespeare has a firmer grasp of the problems involved in dramatizing that inadequacy. The next chapter will suggest how language in *Timon of Athens* becomes antithetical and fragmented, as Timon strains to express his growing apprehension of the radically disjunct nature of human experience in his world. Timon's last words will leave no doubt concerning his sense of the impotence of language before an anarchic reality: "Lips, let sour words go by and language end" (V. i. 218)—a

[29] Norman Maclean, "Episode, Scene, Speech and Word: the Madness of Lear," in *Critics and Criticism,* ed. R. S. Crane (Chicago: Univ. of Chicago Press, 1952), p. 614.

sentiment reminiscent of Troilus' "But march away, / Hector is dead; there is no more to say" (V. x. 21–22). In *Lear*, however, the formal control of ultimate extremity allows Shakespeare to coordinate exquisitely anguished actions so as to suggest a valid transcendence of verbal representation. His understanding of the disjunction between language and extreme suffering is perhaps most explicitly stated when Edgar, coming suddenly upon his blinded father, exclaims in shocked disbelief, "The worst is not / So long as we can say 'This is the worst'" (IV. i. 27–28). The emphasis here, as Burckhardt suggests,[30] should fall on the word "say," for Edgar is brutally compelled to acknowledge what the rest of us have been gradually learning: that in this play "the worst" is a condition of suffering beyond the capacities of language. When Edgar later observes the "side-piercing sight" of the mad king's grotesque encounter with his father, he seems to feel himself very close to that speechless condition: "I would not take this from report—it is, / And my heart breaks at it" (IV. vi. 139–40). The pity and terror communicated by the tableau before him can only be suggested indirectly and negatively by recourse to the neutral pointer "it." By the end of the play even this most slight concession to language is apparently an unacceptable compromise when we confront the full reality of human grief. When Lear appears at the end of the play carrying Cordelia's body, he underscores the only allowable use of words remaining in a universe that can sanction such meaningless destruction.

> Howl, howl, howl! O, you are men of stones.
> Had I your tongues and eyes, I'ld use them so
> That heaven's vault should crack.
> (V. iii. 258–60)

By reliance on euphemisms such as "it" and "this," together with the simple muteness of various characters when confronted by unutterable instances of cruelty, Shakespeare uses his medium to flood our consciousness with the apprehension of a nameless, fundamental horror: "a deed without a name." During the mad scenes in Act III, language almost completely loses its primary communicative function as Shakespeare endows Edgar, Lear, and the Fool with a fractured syntax and disjointed dialogue that tend to reduce language to mere sounds and gestures.[31] Similarly, Lear's behavior in Act IV, scene 6

[30] Burckhardt, p. 253.
[31] Kolve speaks of this scene as "a kind of fugue for three mad voices" (p. 179). Harley Granville-Barker says of moments such as this that "the sound of the dialogue matters almost more than its meaning" (p. 294).

reveals that in his crazed mind words have assumed, as Burckhardt puts it, "a phonetic corporeality that strips them of meaning."[32] Shakespeare can also create an effect that goes beyond language by occasionally using words in an extremely elaborate and periphrastic manner, as in Kent's amplified description of Oswald's knavery (II. ii. 10–31). He also constructs a wordy and radically disjunctive simile in order to suggest the supra-linguistic nature of Goneril's and Regan's lavish cruelty. Witness how Albany struggles to find words to express Goneril's monstrous ingratitude to her father.

> A father, and a gracious agèd man,
> Whose reverence even the head-lugged bear would lick,
> Most barbarous, most degenerate, have you madded.
> (IV. ii. 41–43)

Notice how the unreality, the utter impossibility of what has somehow actually happened, appears at least two removes from direct expression and human understanding: only under the most extreme conditions, if at all, would it become conceivable that a "head-lugged bear" would "lick" even the most reverend head. It thus becomes still more incomprehensible that under the same extreme conditions a daughter would actually turn her "gracious" old father out. The comparison points to a middle term that is beyond comprehension, for to grasp the extent of Goneril's evil nature, the simile obliquely tells us, we must pass beyond language (man's defining characteristic) to a wordless monstrous reality. As Lear runs from the stage in Act IV crowned with poisonous weeds and babbling incoherently, a Gentleman exclaims, "A sight most pitiful in the meanest wretch, / Past speaking of in a king" (IV. vi. 200–01). Again we experience the insufficiency of language —a denial of the adequacy of the superlative in regard to certain ultra-extreme situations. By the recurrent use of such striking locutions involving animals we can contemplate bestial behavior far beyond the reach of direct expression. Gloucester admonishes Regan, "If wolves had at thy gate howled that stern time [of Lear's exposure on the heath], / Thou shouldst have said, 'Good porter, turn the key'" (III. vii. 63–64). Since it is extremely unlikely that Regan would befriend a "wolf," how much more beyond comprehension, then, that under the same conditions she would banish her own father. It is left for Cordelia to urge this peculiar idiom beyond its "outermost mark." On hearing of Lear's cruel treatment, she exclaims in shocked disbelief:

[32] Burckhardt, p. 251.

> Mine enemy's dog,
> Though he had bit me, should have stood that night
> Against my fire; and wast thou fain, poor father,
> To hovel thee with swine and rogues forlorn
> In short and musty straw?
> (IV. vii. 36–40)

Cordelia's construction of outrage out-tops the extremity of the other similes examined, since the sequence of improbability now runs from "enemy" to "enemy's dog" to "enemy's dog [that] had bit me"—three removes from the possible! These hyperbolic similes are not obtrusive, but they join with the other linguistic strategies mentioned previously to create a general sense of how language can paradoxically transcend its own limitations.

IV

We have seen how the plot, scenario, and language of *King Lear* operate in consort to extend the boundaries of poetic drama and to intensify the play's emotional impact. The most difficult aspect of the play's design, however, is characterization—in particular, the character of the protagonist and the nature of his interdependence with the various people who surround and support him. Royal Lear seems to top extremity in almost every respect: from his great age (his "fourscore and upward" is just vague enough to suggest an age far beyond ordinary longevity) to what Granville-Barker describes as the "megalithic grandeur" of his majestic bearing.[33] We recall how his ability to project and sustain a larger than life dramatic image provoked Charles Lamb's warning that no actor should attempt to represent Lear's force and magnitude: "they might more easily propose to personate the Satan of Milton upon a stage, or one of Michael Angelo's terrible figures."[34] The critical prejudices of our own age have occasionally caused some commentators to regard Lear as not so much a human being as "a great tangled web of poetic images and philosophical concepts."[35] After having conceived a figure of such massive proportions, Shakespeare compels him to undergo a protracted trial, the

[33] Granville-Barker, p. 271.
[34] Charles Lamb, "On Shakespeare's Tragedies" (1808), from *The Complete Works in Prose and Verse of Charles Lamb* (London: Chatto and Windus, 1875), p. 261.
[35] Alan Brien, "Openings: London," *Theatre Arts,* 47 (1963), 58.

unbearable length and agony of which places him even further beyond the pale of familiar human experiences. We agree with Kent's assessment that "The tyranny of the open night's too rough / For nature to endure" (III. iv. 2–3), but still Lear does endure. Even the unusually beleaguered survivors of the play's tragic action must conclude that "The oldest hath borne most; we that are young / Shall never see so much, nor live so long" (V. iii. 326–27).

Emphasis on grandeur and heroic endurance severely strains the resources of stage and actor. The most challenging aspect, however, both conceptually and formally, of Lear's character is this: the exquisitely prolonged torture and anguish Lear suffers generate passion of such great intensity that it actually seems to disintegrate his initial regal selfhood and to drive him through several rather clearly articulated transformations. The Fool's comment, "This cold night will turn us all to fools and madmen" (III. iv. 75), hints at how the process of decomposition will work—as does Cordelia's reference to Lear as "this child-changèd father!" (IV. vii. 17). By the end of the play Lear will have lived through a variety of answers to his question, "Who is it that can tell me who I am?" (I. iv. 220). Perhaps nowhere is Shakespeare's bold attempt to expand the capacities of his medium more apparent than in his experimentation with characterization in this play.

The relation between serious psychic disturbance and transformation of character is a curious feature of several Shakespearean plays.[36] The general sense of fundamental breakdown in *Troilus and Cressida,* for instance, causes characterization to be uncommonly precarious and at times even contradictory, so that Troilus can properly exclaim, "This is, and is not, Cressid" (V. ii. 142). In *Hamlet* Claudius informs Rosencrantz and Guildenstern of "Hamlet's transformation," explaining that "nor th' exterior nor the inward man / Resembles that it was" (II. ii. 5–7). With some understatement Iago describes the "noble Moor," who strikes and insults Desdemona in public, as "much changed" (IV. i. 261). And in the nihilistic world of *Timon of Athens* the protagonist's character is radically transformed from universal altruism to unqualified hatred. "I am Misanthropos and hate mankind" declares "transformèd Timon" in Act IV. That a character may undergo physical and psychic transformation when subjected to extreme emo-

[36] I have been aided in my examination of the dramatic presentation of psychic change and transformation in Shakespearean drama by Maynard Mack's fine essay, "The Jacobean Shakespeare: Some Observations on the Construction of the Tragedies," in *Jacobean Theatre,* ed. John Russell Brown and Bernard Harris (London: Edward Arnold, 1960), pp. 11–41.

tional stress is an idea deriving primarily from Ovid's *Metamorphoses,* and that Ovidian concept has more relevance to the interplay between character and action in *Lear* than is immediately apparent. One way to see and appreciate Shakespeare's handling of transformation in *Lear* is to place it beside *Titus Andronicus* a clearly Ovidian tragedy in several ways remarkably like *Lear.* H. T. Price's exhaustive study of *Titus* concludes with the declaration that "the closest parallel of *Titus* is the plot of *Lear,*" and the New Arden editor of *Titus,* J. C. Maxwell, finds that Titus' "resemblance to Lear is even more striking" than his resemblance to other protagonists.[37] What Lear and the old Roman general most clearly share is a participation in ultra-extreme experiences, which lead finally to madness and a deterioration of being. In both instances Shakespeare's problem is to accommodate that experience to the exigencies of poetic drama.

Both Titus and Lear go mad as a consequence of extraordinary suffering, and they are both caught up in the kind of progression examined earlier, which takes people through ever deepening horrors until they finally break under the burden. The insupportable nature of the cumulation of griefs that gradually overwhelm Titus is the constant motif of Act III, scene 1, of the earlier play. First, his two remaining sons (Lucius having fled) are led off to execution; then, while Titus is lamenting this particular misfortune, Marcus enters and presents to Titus the raped and terribly mutilated Lavinia. Marcus says:

> Titus, prepare thy agèd eyes to weep
> Of if not so, thy noble heart to break!
> I bring consuming sorrow to thine age.
> (III. i. 59–61)

Titus' response to the threat of "consuming sorrow" strikes the keynote for the emerging pattern of suffering beyond extremity. "My grief was at the height before thou cam'st, / And now like Nilus it disdainth bounds" (III. i. 70–71). Titus' sufferings, however—like Lear's in Act II —are only beginning. Aaron enters and persuades Titus to cut off his hand in order to save his sons' lives. Titus complies, but the growing incoherence of his subsequent lamentation causes Marcus to exclaim, "O brother, speak with possibility, / And do not break into these deep extremes" (III. i. 214–15). But Titus is beginning to perceive that "deep extremes" do not apply to his case; he answers, "Is not my sorrow

---

[37] H. T. Price, "The Authorship of *Titus Andronicus,*" JEGP, 42 (1943), 55–81. J. C. Maxwell, ed. The New Arden *Titus Andronicus* (Cambridge, Mass.: Harvard Univ. Press, 1963), p. xi.

deep, having no bottom? / Then be my passions bottomless with them!" (III. i. 216–17). As Edgar will do later, Titus discovers that in certain situations there is no "worst." The passion of this bleak moment is topped when Aaron abruptly returns to present Titus with both his recently severed hand and the heads of his two sons. Now understandably close to madness, Titus exclaims:

> Now let hot Etna cool in Sicily,
> And be my heart an ever-burning hell!
> These miseries are more than may be borne.
> (III. i. 241–43)

Even the previously moderate Marcus adds, "Ah, now no more will I control thy griefs: / . . . Now is a time to storm" (III. i. 259–63). After that series of brutal blows and at this moment of unendurable passion Titus suddenly undergoes an Ovidian transformation from a tearful old general to a mad and calculating revenger: a metamorphosis clearly marked by his long silence and sudden incongruous and diabolic laugh, "Ah, ah, ah!" At the end of the play Marcus recapitulates the pattern of suffering and transformation when he pleads pardon for Titus' inhuman actions, calling them "These wrongs unspeakable, past patience, / Or more than any living man could bear" (V. iii. 126–27). The urge to drive the action beyond extremity into indescribable areas of human grief "past patience" where the character's identity undergoes sudden change makes *Titus* surprisingly similar to *Lear*.

      Shakespeare intends us to understand that, at this moment in Act III, Titus has been transformed into an essentially new identity. The challenge facing him is to make the change dramatically viable.[38] However, *Titus* collapses structurally at this point because Shakespeare seems rather naively to have misjudged the nature of his medium. He appears determined, as Eugene Waith puts it, "to take over part of an Ovidian conception which cannot be fully realized by the techniques of drama." [39] Hence Waith's conclusion that "in *Titus Andronicus* we have the many speeches insisting upon what is extraordinary in the situation of the hero—what makes it beyond human endurance—but the final transformation which would complete the suggestion cannot take place. . . . the action frustrates, rather than reenforces, the operation of

[38] Norman Rabkin, *Shakespeare and the Common Understanding* (New York: The Free Press, 1967), says: "Titus transforms himself into something new, a revenger, a hero-villain, a man as much sinning as sinned against" (p. 253).
[39] Eugene Waith, "The Metamorphosis of Violence in *Titus Andronicus*," *Shakespeare Survey*, 10 (1957), 48.

the poetry." [40] Waith's analysis of *Titus'* formal and conceptual short-comings is perceptive, but his general assessment of the capacities of the Elizabethan stage—and in particular its ability to dramatize character transformation—fails to take account of the fact that fifteen years after the blunders of *Titus* Shakespeare again took up the problems of dramatizing unendurable suffering leading to character transformation, and that in *Lear* he realized a victory for poetic drama.

The principal reason for Shakespeare's achievement in this difficult area of dramaturgy lies in his initial conception of his hero Lear. The majestic old king is a focal character of such unusual power and complexity that he is capable, when subjected to extreme suffering, of generating sub-characters—variations, in part, of his essential self—who allow for the temporal revelation of Lear's manifold personality and experience.[41] The well-known manner in which characters in *Lear* fall into the opposed categories of good and bad becomes understandable when we recognize the essentially allegorical technique of character disposition. Some of the sub-characters, who spring into being from Lear's passion, will naturally seek to aid his best interests; others will group to oppose them. Because of this muted sense of Lear's potent centrality we gradually acquire the feeling that the old sovereign is, in part, actually creating and peopling the world of the play by his initial actions. Burgundy and the King of France, for example, appear at the end of the first scene to dramatize Lear's folly regarding Cordelia's worth. As Lear progresses through the play, and as his passion increases beyond the limits of human endurance, he—unlike his predecessor Titus—continues to generate composite characters of a simpler, autonomous quality who provide palpable commentary on his gradual disintegration.

[40] Ibid.

[41] I have found two works particularly helpful in my study of this dimension of *Lear*'s structure: Angus Fletcher, *Allegory: The Theory of a Symbolic Mode* (Ithaca, N. Y.: Cornell Univ. Press, 1964), and Maynard Mack's aforementioned essay, "The Jacobean Shakespeare." See especially Fletcher's first chapter, "The Daemonic Agent," pp. 35–38. "A systematically complicated character," Fletcher says, "will generate a large number of other protagonists who react against or with him in a syllogistic manner. I say 'generate,' because the heroes of Dante and Spenser and Bunyan seem to create the worlds about them" (p. 36). The value of Mack's essay is in his lucid ability to show how the symbolic mode functions in the structure of Shakespearean tragedy. He shows how a tragic protagonist "will normally pass through a variety of mirroring situations . . . and in some of these, the hero will be confronted, so to speak, with a version of his own situation" (p. 35). I have found Mack's observations on *Lear* particularly helpful. There is also a good discussion of mirroring characters in Francis Fergusson's chapter on *Hamlet*, pp. 127–41.

One reason Lear is forced to move about so much in the course of the play is that such a pilgrimage enables him to keep encountering discrete images of himself.[42]

As Lear moves towards madness and visions of nothingness he continually interacts with people whose principal function is to offer dramatic incarnations of the various levels of psychic derangement through which he passes. Act III of *Lear* is somewhat like Act III of *Titus* in that both protagonists suffer an accelerating series of misfortunes, which, as they accumulate, eventually drive them into insanity. However, *Lear* succeeds in dramatically validating that drift by providing visual surrogates for the psychic transformations through which the king passes on his way to madness. Moreover, Shakespeare finds those psychic images in the immediate world Lear has brought into being. "The storm, the Fool, and Poor Tom," as Norman Maclean eloquently puts it, "are not only variations on madness but happenings on the way which collectively constitute the event. That is, the setting and two characters, all previously somewhat external to Lear, successively become objects of his thought, and then himself transubstantiated. We know Lear, thus, by Lear's other substances, which are dramatically visible." [43] In a similar manner Lear comes to know himself as well. The impoverished beggar and madman who appears to him in Act III is not merely Poor Tom, nor even Edgar in clever disguise, but a valid reflection of what Lear himself has become.

To speak of other characters as projections of Lear's decomposing self risks violating the autonomy and obvious psychological realism those characters manifest in the play. But such a risk is unavoidable in dealing with a dramatist whose genius reveals itself in the ability to create *dramatis personae* who readily fuse deep psychological realism with complex quasi-allegorical interrelationships.[44] Even a critic as dedi-

---

[42] Fletcher, pp. 36–37. "Another natural hero for allegory is the traveller, because on his journey he is plausibly led into numerous fresh situations, where it seems likely that new aspects of himself may be turned up." "Shakespearean plotting tends to call for journeys," Mack says in "The Jacobean Shakespeare." "For one thing, journeys can enhance our impression that psychological changes are taking place" (p. 35).

[43] Maclean, p. 605.

[44] Alvin B. Kernan says, "In the greatest Elizabethan drama the tension between formalism and realism is at a maximum. Even in the most 'realistic' plays the characters will often be grouped in the stiff configurations of the morality play. . . . The known and the unknown, the general scheme and the particular individual, these elements compose the great counterpoint of Elizabethan drama" (p. 59).

cated to naturalistic interpretation as A. C. Bradley has to acknowledge in *King Lear* an allegorical configuration based on decomposition partially governing the disposition of the characters. When he considers the *dramatis personae* as a totality, he finds that most of them have little psychological complexity: in fact, "it is not quite natural to us to regard them from this point of view at all." That intuition leads him to suggest that "we seem to trace the tendency, which, a few years later produced Ariel and Caliban, the tendency of the imagination to analyze and abstract, to decompose human nature into its constituent factors." [45] However, Bradley quickly abandons that potentially seminal insight, preferring the certainties of his more customary analysis of character to the difficulties of sustaining a dual awareness of action and character.

Bradley's adherence to a naturalistic criterion implies that character disintegration and the symbolic projection of such deterioration are dangerously incompatible with psychological realism and basic dramatic realities. But this view is surely too narrow for poetic drama. Decomposition of character occurs in *Lear* not because Shakespeare nostalgically accentuates the nearly dormant medieval allegorical mode of characterization, but rather because the ultra-extreme nature of his protagonist's experience makes such fragmentation and refraction of identity both necessary and psychologically meaningful. The coupling of states beyond extremity with decomposition of self, we should note, is also closely related to other formal peculiarities in *Lear*'s structure. We discussed earlier, for instance, how Shakespeare forces language past its normal capacities, explodes its declarative powers, and then relies on the smallest and most inexpressive forms of language—such as "it," "this," and "here"—in order to hint at qualities of feeling and suffering that defy linguistic articulation. In a similar manner Shakespeare causes Lear's initial character to decompose under the extreme pressure of his suffering and then, as Maynard Mack sees it, "uses the stripped-down constituents of personality to point to complexities of being and human reality that lie beyond the scope of ordinary conventions of dramatic character." [46] By focusing on areas of *Lear*'s structure beyond the reach of Bradleian analysis, Maclean and Mack are able to illuminate a dimension of Shakespeare's artistry we are just beginning to understand.

Lear's ability to generate surrogates, who reflect the various qualities involved in his gradual dissolution, appears perhaps most clearly in his relationship to his three daughters. The initial disturbance

[45] Bradley, pp. 263–64.
[46] Mack, *"King Lear" in Our Time,* p. 99.

and imbalance in the old king's capacious self unfold dramatically into the asymmetrical grouping of one good daughter against two bad ones. Although Kent believes "one self mate and make could not beget / Such different issues" (IV. iii. 34–35), Lear himself has to admit that " 'twas this flesh begot / Those pelican daughters" (III. iv. 72–73) Goneril and Regan as well as his "best object" Cordelia. Given the symbolic orientation between parent and offspring, Lear's progress through the play may seem a dynamic working out of propensities for good and evil coexisting in him from the outset. Hence Elton's provocative suggestion that "Lear may be said sequentially to dissociate into his children, Goneril and Regan (selfish wilfulness) and Cordelia (courageous adamancy), as Gloucester may be seen successively to dissolve into his components, Edmund (lust) and Edgar (pathos)." [47] Lear's decline, however, brings him into contact with more aspects of himself than are available in this familial configuration. For instance, consider the manner in which the Fool first appears in the play as a projection of Lear's evolving response to his deteriorating essence. Shakespeare carefully synchronizes the Fool's entrance with the gradual welling up into Lear's consciousness of his own foolishness and of his uncertainty concerning his real identity. Throughout Act I, scene 4 we are repeatedly invited to associate Lear and his Fool as part of one central complex. "The Fool thus serves, to some extent," Mack says, "as a screen on which Shakespeare flashes, as it were, readings from the psychic life of the protagonist, possibly even his subconscious life, which could not otherwise be conveyed in drama at all." [48] Likewise, the blind and mutilated Gloucester, who stands before Lear in Act IV, scene 6, becomes more than just a figure somewhat analogous to him. He also mirrors back to the mad king a vivid image of what Lear has now become. "If thou wilt weep my fortunes," Lear says, "take my eyes" (IV. vi. 173). The subtle gesture of exchange recalls the Fool's "Here's my coxcomb" (I. iv. 90) and makes essentially the same point about identification.

A more complex screen, on which Shakespeare can project the initial scope and subsequent breakdown of Lear's psychic life, is present in the rather mysterious hundred knights who play such a curious role in the first two acts. To Goneril they are merely part of Lear's "insolent retinue / [Who] hourly carp and quarrel" (I. iv. 192–93), but

---

[47] Elton, p. 280. R. B. Heilman also has some good things to say about how sons and daughters reflect aspects of their parents, *This Great Stage: Image and Structure in "King Lear"* (Baton Rouge, La.: Louisiana State Univ. Press, 1948), pp. 33–36.
[48] Mack, "The Jacobean Shakespeare," p. 24.

to Lear they are "men of choice and rarest parts, / That all particulars of duty know" (254–55). Since we never see them, their actual worth can never be established dramatically. Indeed, their very ambiguity is what makes them of use to Shakespeare. The knights appear to reflect the symbolic complexity of Lear in a manner faintly reminiscent of the "shadow-substance" bond between Lord Talbot and his knights in Act II, scene 3 of *1 Henry VI*. There, in a rather crude and heavy-handed way, the Countess of Auvergne sees that the heroic Talbot's true identity is not limited to his creatural appearance but also extends to include his knights. "Are you now persuaded," Talbot says as his knights surround him, "That Talbot is but shadow of himself?/ These [i.e., his knights] are his substance, sinews, arms, and strength" (II. iii. 62–63). In *King Lear,* however, the "substance" Talbot confidently displays and celebrates has become a concept much more difficult to sustain. At the play's beginning, as Alfred Harbage notes, Lear steps forth as King in an archetypal sense, symbolizing Mankind at the farthest expanse of his powers.[49] His royal substance manifests itself not only in his bearing and speech but also in his concern for his hundred knights—one hundred, in this case, probably because of the number's connotations of wholeness and perfection to the Medieval-Renaissance imagination.[50] The shadowy

[49] Granville-Barker also calls attention to the magnitude of Lear as a protagonist (p. 284), but the best statement of this aspect of Lear's character still remains that of Alfred Harbage in his "Introduction" to the Pelican edition of the play, *William Shakespeare: The Complete Works* (Baltimore, Md.: Penguin Books, 1969). After discussing the "magnitude and force" of the "Titan" we meet as the play opens, he says: "Here is no soft-brained *Senex,* but the archetypal *King.* As such Lear symbolizes Mankind, and we will say nothing essential about him by reckoning up his years and growing glib about the symptoms of senile dementia. The king-figure surrogate is an understandable product of the human mind in its early attempts at abstraction, since the most imposing of single men best lends his image to the difficult concept of Man" (p. 1062).

[50] The most concise and reliable study of numerical symbolism in the Medieval and Renaissance periods can be found in E. R. Curtius' *European Literature and the Latin Middle Ages,* trans. Willard R. Trask (New York: Pantheon Books, 1953). He succinctly surveys the subject in two brief excursuses entitled "Numerical Composition" (pp. 501–09) and "Numerical Apothegms" (pp. 510–14). Curtius points out the special importance of the number 100, showing how the popularity of the number manifests itself in "the elaborate harmony of Dante's numerical composition" of the *Commedia.* "From the enneads of the *Vita Nuova* Dante proceeded to the elaborate numerical structure of the *Commedia:* $1 + 33 + 33 + 33 = 100$ cantos conduct the reader through 3 realms, the last of which contains 10 heavens. Triads and decades intertwine into unity. Here number is no longer an outer framework, but a symbol of the cosmic *ordo*" (p. 509). Curtius adds that "in the Renaissance 100 is popular as a compositional

dramatic existence of those knights tends to qualify Lear's proposed symbolic extension. Still, the initial analogical relationship between the king and his knights allows Shakespeare to strengthen the emphasis on Lear's diminution simply by having them gradually stripped from him by Goneril and Regan in Act II. The basically ontological relationship between Lear and the figure "100" also serves as a necessary context for the Fool's persistent harping on Lear's reduction to nothing.

> Thou wast a pretty fellow when thou hadst no need to care
> for her frowning. Now thou are an O without a figure. I
> am better than thou art now: I am a fool, thou art nothing.
> (I. iv. 182–85)

Like Talbot Lear without his knights will become "but shadow of himself." The Fool emphasizes the point when he answers Lear's question, "Who is it that can tell me who I am?" with the curt and precise "Lear's shadow" (220–21). In a manner that possibly defeats analysis much of *King Lear* exists as reflecting shadows of Lear's central experience.

V

Lear's intricate relationships with other characters—especially with his hundred knights—illustrate his extremely complex dramatic image and also reveal his unique power to people his crowded play-world with fragments of his splintering identity. Moreover, Shakespeare orchestrates those vital interactions in order to keep before us the possibility that Lear will, as he had warned Goneril, "resume the shape which thou dost think / I have cast off for ever" (I. iv. 300–301). As Kent bears Lear away towards Dover and the awaiting Cordelia, for instance, we learn that "Some five or six and thirty of his knights, / Hot questrists after him, met him at gate" (III. vii. 15–16). When Cordelia begins her counter-effort to restore the broken and distracted king to his initial symbolic expansiveness, she does so by dispatching a search party of one hundred men with the suggestive command, "A century send forth!" (IV. iv. 6). But Lear, unlike Talbot, is never to be united with his

---

number: Pacifico Massimi, *Hecatelegium* (1489); Thomas Watson, *The Hekatompathia* or *Passionate Century of Love* (1582); Spenser, *The Tears of the Muses* (1590) with 600 lines" (p. 508). We could add Boccaccio's *Decameron* and Cinthio's *Hecatomithi*. The point is that 100 was understood structurally as a wholeness capable of containing the individual parts of the composition. Shakespeare uses the concept ontologically.

knightly substance. Once under Cordelia's care Lear can again be situated on the chair of state and reinvested with the symbols of his lost sovereignty. But Cordelia's very insistence on his royalty ("my royal lord," "your Majesty," "your Highness") underscores the futility of her hope for a recovery of his former wholeness. He is attired in the fresh garments of kingship, but now they seem to hang like a giant's robe upon his diminished frame. "Pray, do not mock me," Lear tells his solicitous daughter, "I am a very foolish fond old man" (IV. vii. 59–60). Indeed it appears from his baffled comments—"all the skill I have / Remembers not these garments" (66–67)—that the regal concepts symbolized by dress and deference are now alien to him. Lear does achieve a reconciliation with Cordelia, of course, but their purely private reunion falls short of the public restoration of dignity she desires for her king-father. If we share her partial disappointment as she helps him from the stage, we may also glimpse the dismal sequence of defeat, imprisonment, and death quickly to follow for them.

Left finally in that "cheerless, dark, and deadly" (V. iii. 291) atmosphere of the play's conclusion, with its exhausted speech rhythms and stark tableaus of grief, we may feel we have arrived at last at the area of experience "beyond extremity" and towards which all elements of *Lear* have been moving. Kent's cry, "Break, heart, I prithee break!" (313), spoken as Lear's heart, like Gloucester's, finally bursts " 'Twixt two extremes of passion, joy and grief" (199), marks the end of a series of references to heartbreak made by Edgar, Albany, and Kent. In all those speeches, as Reuben Brower notes, " 'riving' imagery is being used of the 'great breach' in nature strained past enduring." [51] Moreover, the art of poetic drama seems itself strained beyond endurance in the presence of what Kent terms "the rack of this tough world" (315). Except possibly for Lear's "Never, never, never, never, never" (309), there is no more to say. It is appropriate that Edgar, the artificer of ordered perspectives and consoling dramas in Act IV, should be the one to close the play with the acknowledgment that "The weight of this sad time we must obey" (323). There will be "no play / To ease the anguish of [this] torturing hour" (*MND*. V. i. 36–37), for we have been taken into the realm of a "naturalism" seemingly beyond all artistic formulation. [52] Just as Edgar's imaginative structuring of Dover Cliff made us feel the nothingness out of which it is composed, so here the

[51] Reuben Brower, *Hero and Saint: Shakespeare and the Graeco-Roman Heroic Tradition* (New York and Oxford: Oxford Univ. Press, 1971), p. 414.
[52] Burckhardt says, "In Shakespeare—in fact in poetic drama—I know of no 'naturalism' to equal the end of this play" (p. 257).

ostensible inadequacy of art makes us feel even more directly the unspeakable experience before us. To recognize the scope of that achievement is to dismiss all bothersome thoughts about *Lear*'s artistic greediness or lack of control. Perhaps we will always feel, as Coleridge did, that "the tragic in this play has been urged beyond the outermost mark and *ne plus ultra* of the dramatic," but we shall more clearly grasp the spirit of *King Lear* if such a feeling moves us to praise rather than to reproach.

V CONFOUNDING CONTRARIES:

The Unmediated World of *Timon of Athens*

❧

The middle of humanity thou never knewest, but the extremity of both ends. (IV. iii. 299–300)

Even in our troubled century *Timon of Athens* has not attracted many admirers. Still, we are less willing than we once were to
take our critical departure from the admonishment carved on Timon's
gravestone: "Pass by and curse thy fill; but pass, and stay not here
thy gait" (V. iv. 73). Timon's harsh gesture of radical disengagement
makes us wonder just what affinity Shakespeare could have glimpsed
between the misanthrope's rhetorical stance and the expansive, though
finally limited, capabilities of his medium. No contraries would appear
to hold more antipathy, as Kent might say, than such an antisocial
knave and the dynamic interdependence characteristic of poetic drama.[1]
At the height of his powers Shakespeare seems to be making more
audacious formal demands on his craft than ever before: demands
impossible to realize and made perhaps for that reason.

We should not underestimate the play's deficiencies. For
instance, our curiosity should only be intensified by the repeated demonstrations of the play's unfinished quality,[2] since they compel us to ask

[1] In his "Introduction" to The Pelican Shakespeare edition of *Timon of Athens*
(Baltimore, Md.: Penguin Books, 1964), Charlton Hinman charges that Shakespeare "fails to make Timon himself an entirely satisfactory protagonist" (p. 27).
"Timon's response to misfortune is not only unheroic but undramatic," Hinman
says. "Dust and heat—involvement and conflict—are the life-blood of drama,"
and Timon "simply withdraws from the world of men" (p. 26).
[2] I can offer only a brief sampling of this entrenched attitude towards *Timon's*
formal peculiarities. E. K. Chambers, *William Shakespeare: A Study of Facts*

exactly how such a dramatic undertaking—given the baffling misalliance of content and form—could have ever been finished satisfactorily. Shakespeare could not have eradicated the problems in the play simply by correcting the inconsistencies in the spelling of names, by smoothing out metrical irregularities, or by eventually getting straight the precise worth of a Greek talent.[3] A more solid basis for criticism is A. C. Bradley's observation that "though care might have made it clear, no mere care could make it really dramatic,"[4] since he correctly implies that observable structural flaws are really more a matter of conception than formal execution. However, the once common line of approach that tried to account for that apparent misconception by regarding the play as "an exercise in purgation, personal to Shakespeare rather than dramatically controlled" no longer commands much assent either.[5] The naive assumption that Timon, in his fury, represents the catastrophic release of some fundamental disturbance in Shakespeare's soul grossly ignores the critical distance Shakespeare sustains between himself and his raging protagonist. The time has passed when the perplexed critic could dismiss the play either as an odd instance of perverse dramaturgy or as an embarrassing occasion of personal breakdown. Nor can it be reasonably argued, as G. W. Knight tries to do, that in its achieved perfection *Timon* "includes and transcends" Shakespeare's great tragedies.[6] Its bold and damaging experimentation—

---

and Problems (Oxford: Oxford Univ. Press, 1930), vol. 1, p. 481, says "I do not doubt that it was left unfinished by Shakespeare, and I believe that the real solution of its 'problem,' indicated long ago by Ulrici and others, is that it is unfinished still." Una Ellis-Fermor, "*Timon of Athens:* An Unfinished Play," RES, 18 (1942), 270–83, quotes Chambers with approval and concludes her fine study with the comment: "It *is* unfinished in this way also, it is true. But, what matters more, it is unfinished in conception" (p. 282). See also Terence Spencer, "Shakespeare Learns the Value of Money: The Dramatist at Work on *Timon of Athens," Shakespeare Survey,* 6 (1953), 75–78, and Hinman's remarks in his "Introduction," pp. 20–25, in the aforementioned edition, to the play.

[3] There is a thorough discussion of all these "inconsistencies and loose ends" in H. J. Oliver's excellent "Introduction" to The New Arden edition of *Timon of Athens* (Cambridge, Mass.: Harvard Univ. Press, 1959), pp. xiv–xvi.

[4] A. C. Bradley, *Shakespearean Tragedy: Lectures on "Hamlet," "Othello," "King Lear," "Macbeth"* (London: Macmillan, 1904, reprinted, 1967), p. 245. Bradley deigns to comment on *Timon* only in several scattered footnotes, but his brief observations are often valuable.

[5] This particular phrase is Donald A. Stauffer's, *Shakespeare's World of Images: The Development of His Moral Ideas* (New York: W. W. Norton, 1949), p. 227, but it should be taken as merely representative of a widely dispersed and often repeated point of view.

[6] See the highly subjective essay, "The Pilgrimage of Hate: An Essay on *Timon*

its sensitivity to the divisive tendencies in poetic drama—does not associate it with those masterpieces but rather with the supposed dramatic failures like *Troilus and Cressida* and *Measure for Measure*: plays that relinquish popularity and formal coherence to more pressing artistic imperatives. *Timon of Athens* is not an isolated phenomenon in the Shakespeare canon but another of those moments of radical scrutiny into the nature and potentiality of the dramatic medium. Before we can pursue this hypothesis, however, we need to briefly summarize the relationship of the dramatist to his medium.

I

More than other artists the poetic dramatist is at the mercy of circumstances over which he can exercise little control, since he must communicate his vision to a live audience through a complex synchronization of speech, action, and the interplay of personalities. The peculiar worldliness of the dramatic event forces the playwright to bring forth his subjects on the "unworthy scaffold" and to acquiesce in the judgment of his "fair beholders." His stance, whether he likes it or not, must be that of the "prologue armed" who introduces *Troilus and Cressida* with "Like or find fault; do as your pleasures are: / Now good or bad, 'tis but the chance of war" (Pro. 30–31). Like Prospero he must finally apologize for his "crimes" and beg for his audience's "indulgence" (Epi. 19–20). Shakespeare's acute sensitivity to the mediated nature of his art cannot help but deepen his understanding that a vulnerable between-ness is a condition common to all human relations.[7] His evolving knowledge of his medium is simultaneously an exploration into that aspect of the human condition.

An increasingly somber thread, woven into the variegated

---

of Athens," in G. W. Knight, *The Wheel of Fire: Interpretations of Shakespearian Tragedy* (London: Methuen: 1930, reprinted, 1949), pp. 207–39. "For this play is *Hamlet, Troilus and Cressida, Othello, King Lear*, become self-conscious and universal; it includes and transcends them all" (p. 236). Knight's hyperbolic assessment has found very few seconds.

[7] I am thinking here of the work of Sigurd Burckhardt whose general method is to find "an inner logic in the development of [Shakespeare's] dramatic poetry" by tracing "Shakespeare's gradual, and painful, discovery of his medium and thereby of his own true function and powers." See p. 260 of his excellent essay "The King's Language: Shakespeare's Drama as Social Discovery," *Shakespearean Meanings* (Princeton: Princeton Univ. Press, 1968). Perhaps I should once more acknowledge my general indebtedness to Burckhardt's several essays on Shakespeare and his sense of medium.

fabric of Shakespeare's drama, traces his response to the bondage both of man and artist to processes of mediation. For instance, the happy endings of the comedies written before 1600 are usually brought about by the providential intervention of benevolent agencies, such as Oberon, Portia, Rosalind, and Don Pedro, who exploit staged actions and language to create harmony and peaceful continuity. Yet even those joyous plays can occasionally allow us glimpses of a more ominous potentiality dormant in such comic intercession. Oberon and Puck have good intentions, but that fact does not keep them from indulging at times in a simple delight in the human confusion they half-inadvertently produce. Portia and Rosalind also reveal a penchant for verbal and spectacular theatrics slightly in excess of immediate needs. Don Pedro's benign intervention on behalf of Claudio and Hero is not only confusing in itself but must compete against the devilish agency of his bastard brother Don John. In *Much Ado,* in fact, mediation polarizes into the clear opposition of the two brotherly "practisers," and there is consequently a growing realization here of the negative potential coexisting in all mediated relationships. So that when Don John's vulgar insinuations cause Claudio to misinterpret Don Pedro's efforts on his behalf, the young man can exclaim with some cogency, "Let every eye negotiate for itself / And trust no other agent" (II. i. 176–77). Claudio's aspiration for a self-negotiating, unmediated love relationship is only lightly sounded and quickly abandoned, but his desire is fundamental to the tragic experiences of Romeo and Juliet, Othello and Desdemona, Lear and Cordelia, Antony and Cleopatra, and especially Troilus and Cressida. Indeed, it is in Troilus' prophetic cry, "O gods, how do you plague me! / I cannot come to Cressid but by Pandar" (I. i. 90–91), that we hear most clearly the tragic lament shared by all those death-marked lovers. In the ludicrous figure of the Pandar —that indispensable but grossly inadequate go-between—Shakespeare concentrates his increasing skepticism concerning the legitimacy of the benign mediation which reigns in his comic universe.

In the great tragedies that follow *Troilus and Cressida* the dramatic embodiments of unreliable mediation assume the more clearly demonic forms of Iago, Edmund, and the Weird Sisters: malevolent agencies who now operate uncontestedly and whose interventions produce only separation and death. The necessity of leading mediated lives is no longer a neutral condition capable of both good and evil (as in *Much Ado*); it has become the sign of our inescapable isolation and doom. Benign mediators are now routed by their evil counterparts. We can see in Iago's triumph over Desdemona and in Edmund's easy manipulation of Edgar the belated vengeance of Don John over Don Pedro and his talent for reconciliation. In fact, it is Desdemona's willingness to mediate, her earnest solicitations on Cassio's behalf, that provides the means whereby Iago can "make the net / That shall enmesh them all" (II. iii. 344–45). Those evil intermediaries also function, like Friar Laurence, Pandarus, and Duke Vincentio, as playwrights in their control of their play-worlds. Now, however, Shakespeare uses surrogate figures to sustain a gloomy commentary on his own necessary commitment to artistic strategies of mediation. As a dramatist he knows himself to be an accomplice in the illusory pageants that ensnare Othello and Gloucester, and as a poet he realizes he must bear some responsibility for the ambiguous mediacy of language: its tendency, as Macbeth learns, to "palter with us in a double sense" (V. viii. 20). In the very creation of those plays Shakespeare tacitly acknowledges his own complicity in the evil he brilliantly sets forth. The treacherous mediacy, within which his doomed characters must act, is essentially the same mediacy within which he must struggle for artistic mastery.

Perhaps the most striking feature of the last tragedies— *Antony and Cleopatra, Coriolanus,* and *Timon of Athens*—is the sudden disappearance of the malicious middleman (the playwright surrogate in his negative aspect) from his major role in the play's action. Indeed, those difficult plays seem to have turned away from processes of mediation almost entirely, abandoning their worlds to a self-destructive dialectic involving unarbitrated extremes: Rome versus Egypt, Coriolanus versus Rome, Timon versus all humanity. The potential intermediaries who do still appear are now neither good nor bad but simply pathetically impotent figures like Lepidus and Octavia, Menenius and Virgilia, or Flavius. They are characters whose main function is to illuminate, by their helplessness, the peculiarly bleak kind of world they inhabit. Octavia is offered to Antony and Caesar as the means "To hold you in perpetual amity, / To make you brothers, and to knit your hearts / With an unslipping knot" (II. ii. 125–27), but no one really believes she will succeed. "A more unhappy lady," she is soon lamenting, "ne'er stood between, / Praying for both parts" (III. iv. 12–14). As she finally acquiesces in her inability to arbitrate the widening gap between her husband and her brother, she finds precise expression for her functionless role in the phrase "no midway / 'Twixt these extremes at all (III. iv. 19–20). No villainous agents need appear to generate destructive actions in such a world because the dialectical nature of the unmediated conflicts makes such a catalyst unnecessary and redundant. "The Jove of power make me most weak, most weak, / Your reconciler!" Octavia prays, but her awareness of her ineptitude as a mediator allows her prayer to modulate into a vision of what the world of *Antony and Cleopatra* has been destined to become from the outset:

> Wars 'twixt you twain would be
> As if the world should cleave, and that slain men
> Should solder up the rift.
> (III. iv. 30–32)

Enobarbus takes up and rephrases Octavia's monstrous image of a world split apart when he exclaims, "Then, world, thou hast a pair of chaps, no more; / And throw between them all the food thou hast, / They'll grind the one the other" (III. v. 12–14). We glimpse the radically fragmented worlds of *Antony and Cleopatra* and of *Coriolanus* in such utterances. There is nothing to "solder up the rift" in those worlds but the men slain by its self-destructive warfare. There is no operative middle term.[8] The plays have an austere and uncompromising magnificence, but it is *Timon of Athens* that finally brings to an explosive climax Shakespeare's progression towards a play composed with "no midway."

In both the structure and content of *Timon of Athens* we encounter a persistent refusal to acknowledge any effective form of the mediate. The formal principle guiding the rising structure approximates the syllogistic law of the excluded middle with its rejection of such mediating processes as compromise, modulation, subordination, and continuity. The play stubbornly resists all formal tendencies towards synthesis or fusion, and, therefore, structural units tend to remain disparate, isolated, and paratactic. Shakespeare has abandoned for the

---

[8] Some very good remarks on the centerless nature of *Antony and Cleopatra* can be found in John Danby's fine essay, *"Antony and Cleopatra: A Shakespearean Adjustment,"* in *Poets on Fortune's Hill: Studies in Sidney, Shakespeare, Beaumont and Fletcher* (London: Faber and Faber, 1952), pp. 128–51. "As Caesar impersonates the World, [Cleopatra], of course, incarnates the Flesh. Part of Shakespeare's sleight of hand in the play . . . is to construct an account of the human universe consisting of only these two terms. There is no suggestion that the dichotomy is resolvable" (p. 145). "The World and the Flesh, Rome and Egypt, the two great contraries that maintain and destroy each other, considered apart from any third sphere which might stand over against them," (p. 149) is the basis of the play's structure according to Danby. He is aware of "a missing third term" (p. 149) in the play, and relates it to an absence of effective mediators.

moment his more familiar talent for pitching voice against voice and personality against personality in realistically conceived scenes that are vibrant with complex and dynamic interaction. In place of such anticipated resonance and multiplicity we are confronted with a dramatic texture characterized by stark oppositions and abrupt noncommunicative contrasts and by disturbing disjunctions and harsh antitheses. The most visible example of that general tendency is Timon himself, whose radically disjunct character stands fully illuminated in Apemantus' succinct comment: "The middle of humanity thou never knewest, but the extremity of both ends" (IV. iii. 299–300). In what M. C. Bradbrook aptly calls "this drama of the gaps," [9] Apemantus' phrase transcends its immediate dramatic context and resonates suggestively through the whole design of *Timon of Athens*. It suggests that Shakespeare's determination to avoid the middle ground of compromise and moderation extends far beyond the schizoid personality of his protagonist. The same disjunctive impulse shapes and controls the discontinuous progression of the play's scenario, the puzzling juxtaposition of main plot and subplot, the dislocations in Timon's relations to his Athenian society, the atomism in patterns of imagery and syntax,[10] the strangely bifurcated conclusion of the play, and even the play's difficulty in establishing real communication with its audience. Every element of the play's organization reflects the nonparticipatory stance of the misanthrope.

II

We enter the polarized social world of *Timon of Athens* by observing the unusual manner in which Shakespeare fashions and projects Timon's dramatic image against the backdrop of his Athenian society. That image appears in bold relief, for no other protagonist in the tragedies—not even Coriolanus—so clearly dominates the world

[9] M. C. Bradbrook, *The Tragic Pageant of "Timon of Athens"* (Cambridge: Cambridge Univ. Press, 1966), p. 4.
[10] I have in mind here the studies of syntax and imagery carried out by Una Ellis-Fermor, in her aforementioned article, and by William Empson, in "Timon's Dog," *The Structure of Complex Words* (London: Chatto & Windus, 1951), pp. 175–84. Ellis-Fermor concludes that many of the passages in the play are "merely a succession of units, . . . jottings, thoughts that form in the writer's mind as prosodic units, but not yet related prosodically so as to form a verse paragraph or even a continuous succession of blank verse lines" (p. 275). After a detailed and useful study of the ambivalent meanings suspended in the dog imagery of *Timon*, Empson says that "the striking thing, I think, is that the dog symbolism could be worked out so far and yet remain quite separate" (p. 183).

of his play. From the time of his mock banquet until his death near the play's end Timon monopolizes the stage and speaks well over sixty percent of all the lines. He is the constant focal point of attention from the moment the play begins until its conclusion, and all the action converges on him quasi-magically, like base metal attracted by the magnet. The Poet, who watches the Athenian populace swarm into Timon's palace, opens the play with the astonished exclamation: "Magic of bounty, all these spirits thy power / Hath conjured to attend!" (I. i. 6–7). As he and the Painter talk of Timon's "amplest entertainment," the crowd rapidly increases until the Poet can refer to them as "this confluence, this great flood of visitors" (42). In less than one hundred lines in the first scene there are five separate stage directions indicating entrances, some, such as "Enter Alcibiades with the rest" (244), including a large number of people. Timon is subjected throughout to the varied solicitations of Athenian society, first in his crowded palace in Athens but no less so, curiously enough, in his cave in the wilderness. He even attracts the gold he now despises and is actually richer in the wilderness than he ever was in the city. His last gesture is appropriately an ironic invitation to all "Athens, in the sequence of degree / From high to low throughout" (V. i. 206–07) to visit him one final time in order to "stop affliction" by hanging themselves from his tree. Even after his death there remains his standing command for Athens to "Thither come, / And let my gravestone be your oracle" (V. i. 216–17). Neither in misanthropic withdrawal nor in death does Timon succeed in separating himself from his despised society. "Dead / Is noble Timon," Alcibiades announces as the play concludes, "of whose memory / Hereafter more" (V. iv. 79–81).

Yet Timon never really seems to be an integral part of that society. Nor do we know much about his essential character. Despite his great importance in the play's action Timon reveals far less personality than do such relatively secondary figures as Cassius or Gloucester in other tragedies. Unlike Brutus or Macbeth, Timon is not given to introspection, so we learn practically nothing about his motives either before or after his self-banishment.[11] Indeed, it is difficult to attribute any interior depth, any psychology, to Timon at all. His ontological identity consists almost entirely of his public acts vis-à-vis his community. And although he is in fundamental conflict with that society,

[11] Ellis-Fermor says: "We do not know him and we do not know about him . . . ;" he fails "to leave a deep, coherent impression of his personality," and he lacks "a wide variety of enthusiasms and richness of personality" (pp. 280–81).

he is not endowed with enough being to stand apart from it. Unlike Hamlet he cannot fall back on the ontologically reassuring sense of possessing "that within which passeth show." Hence the play cannot be concerned with exploring that psychologically rich middle ground between self and other that interested Shakespeare in earlier tragedies. Having turned away from mediation, Shakespeare must abandon his former delight in placing his protagonists in threshold situations programmed to reveal an amazingly detailed mimesis of psychological depth and complexity. For instance, we may wonder what kinds of thoughts flood Timon's consciousness during the interval between his naive expressions of absolute confidence in the generosity of his friends —"I am wealthy in my friends" (II. ii. 181)—and his shattering disillusionment. Even here Shakespeare excludes the vital middle and keeps that aspect of Timon's psyche in total eclipse. "His comfortable temper has forsook him," the servant Servilius informs those awaiting Timon's delayed appearance, "he's much out of health and keeps his chamber" (III. iv. 69–71). Timon's spiritual *agon*—his dynamic achievement of insight—takes place behind closed doors, and the new entity who finally comes crashing through those doors crosses, in an explosive instant, the threshold between one identity and another.

We cannot take the general exclamations of rage that fill the second half of the play as revelatory soliloquies, since they don't seem to issue from an established and recognizable personality. As we shall see, they have a disturbingly disembodied quality that partially undermines their power. Even in the earlier urban scenes, however, Shakespeare withholds any information that would permit us to orient Timon either as a unified self or as an integrated member of his immediate community. Instead, Timon's relations, both to the inner world of psychological causality and the outer world of social interactions, are marked by a radical polarization. For all their seeming familiarity Timon and the Athenians face each other over a void. There is absolutely no acknowledgment in the depiction of their relationship of the various social spheres and institutions that ordinarily function as important mediating levels in man's accommodation with his society. For instance, *Timon*'s world is unique in its strict avoidance of wives, children, or even kinsmen. In fact, the only women in the play, aside from the masculine Amazons who appear briefly in the masque, are the two diseased prostitutes who accompany Alcibiades on his campaign against Athens. The absence of the familial bond suggests that no one in the unmediated world of the play is organically related to another person. Even though *Timon*'s focus is severely communal throughout, the basic constituents of a vital functioning society—mutuality and reciprocity—are noticeably lacking from the play.

The nonexistence of organic bonds has crucial significance. It reveals how the familiar Renaissance conception of a unified body politic—a way of mediating the general welfare by situating various members of the state on graduated levels of natural competence—has given way in *Timon of Athens* to a more rigid system of dialectical relationships, which compel individuals to struggle endlessly for a merely personal dominance.[12] Describing the allegorical poem he has written for Timon, the Poet, who opens the play, pictures human relations as primarily a ruthless competition between unrelated individuals, in which all kinds of natures / . . . labor on the bosom of this sphere / To propagate their states" (I. i. 65–67). What is being propagated is not family or society, but pure self-aggrandisement. Personal success, moreover, necessarily involves the subjection, indeed enslavement, of one's competitors. Hence, the Poet's description of how the "present grace" (i. e., sudden monetary good fortune) of his Timon-figure "to present slaves and servants / Translates his rivals" (I. i. 71–72). The balance and repetition in the phrase "present grace to present slaves" encourages us to see the transformation of rivals to slaves as the spontaneous consequence of Timon's acquisition of wealth. As the Poet continues to adumbrate Timon's curious relationship with the Athenians the master-slave configuration becomes even more pronounced. We learn that Timon's prosperity does not add to the general well-being of Athens but rather reduces Timon's former equals and superiors to attitudes of abject subservience.

> All those which were his fellows but of late
> (Some better than his value) on the moment
> Follow his strides, his lobbies fill with tendance,
> Rain sacrificial whisperings in his ear,
> Make sacred even his stirrup, and through him
> Drink the free air.
> (I. i. 78–83)

The ugly bond depicted here between master and slave is the only basis for community in *Timon*. It is clearly based more on envy and

---

[12] In this regard *Timon* is quite similar to *Coriolanus*, a play which also depicts human relations as dialectical rather than organic. *Coriolanus* has been examined from this perspective by Michael McCanles, whose very fine essay, "The Dialectic of Transcendence in Shakespeare's *Coriolanus*," PMLA, 72 (1967), 44–53, has helped me better understand *Timon*.

hate than on love, so it is not surprising that the Poet's allegory ends in a description of the immediate and total desertion of the Timon-figure by his dependents, when suddenly "Fortune in her shift and change of mood / Spurns down her late beloved" (84–85). For such is the heartless logic of an unmediated world where one is either A or not-A, either master or slave. There is no middle.

The Poet's allegory provides a necessary perspective on Timon's initial adulation by exposing the fundamental ambiguity that underlies all his dealings with the Athenians. When Timon himself enters, Shakespeare presents two graphic demonstrations of precisely how Timon's great wealth "Subdues and properties to his love and tendance / All sorts of hearts" (I. i. 57–58). Timon is immediately petitioned, first by a messenger from the imprisoned Ventidius and then by an Old Athenian. In both cases the servile posture of the supplicants illuminates Timon's own greater glory. His generosity in ransoming Ventidius may be sincere, but it only allows Ventidius to exchange one form of bondage for another more subtle form.

> TIMON. I'll pay the debt and free him.
> MESSENGER. Your lordship ever binds him.
> (I. i. 103–04)

Ventidius will soon learn that being imprisoned by Timon's bounty is a more desperate incarceration than debtors' prison. When Ventidius attempts to discharge his debt at the beginning of the next scene, Timon cuts him off with the exclamation:

> O, by no means,
> Honest Ventidius. You mistake my love:
> I gave it freely ever; and there's none
> Can truly say he gives, if he receives.
> (I. ii. 8–11)

The temptation is to see this response as a splendid gesture of Christian *agape,* but to do so is to miss Shakespeare's irony. Timon's liberality here and elsewhere, as Terence Eagleton puts it, "overwhelms, reducing other givers and their gifts to nothing beside itself." [13] Timon responds to the Old Athenian's complaint by enriching the servant Lucilius so he can marry the old man's daughter. Again there is an ominous note of deeper bondage in Lucilius' grateful reply: "Humbly I thank your

[13] See Terence Eagleton's brief remarks on *Timon* in *Shakespeare and Society: Critical Studies in Shakespearean Drama* (New York: Schocken Books, 1967), p. 172.

lordship. Never may / That state or fortune fall into my keeping / Which is not owed to you!" (149–51). Likewise, Timon's response to the gifts of the Poet, Painter, and Jeweller is marred by a sense of personal dominance and subtle corruption. "I like your work, / And you shall find I like it," Timon says. Then comes the inevitable suggestion of enslavement: "Wait attendance / Till you hear further from me" (160–62). This admirable opening scene ends with a summary comment by an anonymous observer concerning the impossibility of any truly reciprocal relationship with Timon: "no gift to him / But breeds the giver a return exceeding / All use of quittance" (275–77).

During the lavish banquet that makes up the second scene Shakespeare shows in more detail how Timon's prodigality works to generate a social environment of intense opposition. The sycophantic Athenians grovel before Timon's magnificence with as much spiteful hate as love, and Timon himself acknowledges their wheedling blandishments with occasional flashes of contempt that foreshadow his latent misanthropy. With understandable petulance one nameless Lord wishes that some kind of reciprocity with Timon were possible for them.

> Might we but have that happiness, my lord, that you
> would once use our hearts, whereby we might express
> some part of our zeals, we should think ourselves for
> ever perfect.
> (I. ii. 79–82)

But the emergent logic of dialectical relationships does not permit Timon to endorse such free-flowing mutuality. The Athenians do not gain whatever worth they possess by their own actions; it is Timon's indiscriminate bounty that confers it on them. "I have told more of you to myself," Timon smugly answers, "than you can with modesty speak in your own behalf; and thus far I confirm you" (87–89). We can perhaps best understand the outrageous blasphemy of Timon's Christ-like behavior here, and elsewhere in this scene, as the measure of his need to transcend his fellow men.[14] Timon appears to use the

---

[14] For a fine discussion of *Timon*'s use of allusions to the *New Testament*, see Jerold W. Ramsey, "Timon's Imitation of Christ," *Shakespeare Studies, 2* (1966), 162–73. Ramsey finds in *Timon* "a pattern of allusions, verbal echoes, and events that has never been adequately dealt with by critics of the play, for one reason or another. It is simply this: in trying to obey the higher 'law' to which he feels bound, Timon becomes a figure of Christ" (p. 165). Other critics have also called attention to the biblical allusions in the play: W. M. Merchant, "*Timon* and the Conceit of Art," *Shakespeare Quarterly, 6* (1955), 249–57, discusses "a group of scriptural references" in Acts I–III, and Winifred

subservience and relative poverty of his guests as an inventory to particularize his own radiant abundance. They, of course, willingly suffer this indignity in order to enrich themselves. Hence, Timon feeds on his guests just as they feed on him, and his effort to play Christ at a communal last supper only spawns contrary images of cannibalism and bestiality.

> O you gods, what a number of men eats Timon, and he sees 'em not! It grieves me to see so many dip their meat in one man's blood; and all the madness is, he cheers them up too.
> (I. ii. 37–40)

In such a society Apemantus' question, "Who lives that's not depravèd or depraves?" (133), has a disturbing aptness.

Despite the close and constant interaction of Timon and the Athenians—their "feasts, pomps, and vainglories" (236)—no sense of true community is present in the play. The hectic give-and-take between patron and clients has only a superficial glitter: a static and lifeless quality that glosses over the essential emptiness and disconnectedness of Athenian existence. All that brings those random members of a disjunct society together is a shared need for the hated "other" as a means of self-definition. With perfectly focused irony Shakespeare brings the banquet scene to its logical conclusion by having Timon and the Athenians exchange syntactically fractured pledges of their full bondage to each other.

> 1. LORD. We are so virtuously bound—
> TIMON.   And so
>   Am I to you.
> 2. LORD.   So infinitely endeared—
> TIMON. All to you.
> (I. ii. 220–22)

Both parties speak truer than they realize. Indeed, that simple and lucid confession of a shared bondage sharply delineates the fundamental nature of human relations in the world of *Timon of Athens*. For both the master and the slave the play will offer no deliverance from the

---

M. T. Nowottny, "Acts IV and V of *Timon of Athens*," *Shakespeare Quarterly*, 10 (1959), 493–97, takes up where Merchant leaves off by showing how inversions of the early scriptural allusions give added meaning to the latter half of the play. See also the comments on communal imagery in *Timon* by Northrop Frye, *Fools of Time: Studies in Shakespearean Tragedy* (Toronto: Univ. of Toronto Press, 1967), pp. 110–11.

rigorous mechanism of that condition short of silence, death, and nothingness. Even in banishment and misanthropy Timon will remain necessarily tied to the society he abhors, and vice versa. Timon's dying words—"nothing brings me all things" (V. i. 186)—will become the inexorable terminus of a social dynamic so carefully established in the opening act.

III

When the steward Flavius announces that "what [Timon] speaks is all in debt; he owes / For every word" (I. ii. 192–93), he both exposes Timon's essential bankruptcy and underscores the sterile nature of discourse in Athenian society. In typical fashion Shakespeare allows the debased quality of the Athenians speech to reflect their moral and cultural impoverishment. The verbal coin of this community, we soon realize, is just as corrupting as the currency it creates and perversely exchanges. Apemantus' presence in the first act seems calculated to make absolutely clear the obscured dishonesties of Athenian fellowship and speech. In his absolute hatred of all parties and in his brutal directness of expression Apemantus emerges as an almost pure distillation of the hostilities latent in the associations between Timon and his countrymen. He first appears just after the Jeweller's fulsome praise of Timon moves the Merchant to say "he speaks the common tongue / Which all men speak with him" (I. i. 174–75), and his immediate task is to lay bare the hypocrisy of this common tongue by uncovering the selfish motives underlying its glib expression. Of the self-serving alliance between Timon and his guests, for instance, Apemantus can say with epigrammatic precision, "He that loves to be flattered is worthy o' th' flatterer" (224).

However, Apemantus himself is only another facet of general Athenian corruption. The ambiguities contained in Timon's communications with his sordid society are more sharply illuminated by the love-hate quality of the cynic's ties to the society he professes to abhor. Apemantus must dog the heels of his fellow men because only in the continued exchanges of mutual contempt can he gauge his own supposed superiority. His repartee with Timon and the Athenians plays constantly on this paradoxical motif.

TIMON. Thou art proud, Apemantus.
APEMANTUS. Of nothing so much as that I am not like Timon.
(I. i. 187–89)

In this regard Apemantus not only hints at the true nature of Timon's love for the Athenians who dutifully act as foils for his splendor, but more importantly he bodies forth the essence of what Timon's misanthropy will be in the second half of the play. When Timon and Apemantus meet again in Act IV, for instance, it will seem, as Kenneth Burke says, as if "Timon were to have fallen into a fantastic quarrel with his mirror-image, under conditions that allowed it to answer back." [15] Indeed, earlier exchanges recur in Act IV in precisely reversed form:

> APEMANTUS.   Art thou proud yet?
> TIMON. Ay, that I am not thee.
> (IV. iii. 276–77)

This depressing reversal reveals just how closed and rigid the diminished universe of *Timon of Athens* actually is. Timon will discover what Apemantus knows from the start: that he can only nourish his self-defining misanthropy on the food he attempts so futilely to do without—other people.

Apemantus' bondage to his enemies is so absolute that, like Timon but in a more literal sense, "what he speaks is all in debt." He must borrow from his society the very words he then uses to castigate it. "How dost thou like this jewel?" Timon asks him. "What dost thou think 'tis worth?" (I. i. 208–11). "Not worth my thinking," Apemantus rejoins, flinging the hated words back on the speaker. The shallowness of the wit reveals the narrow range of verbal abuse available to Apemantus in this stunted society. His expressions of hatred are almost always triggered by the overtures of other people, and it is curious to observe the perverse affection of Timon and the Athenians as they obligingly feed Apemantus the verbal fragments and motifs without which he would be effectively silenced. Still, it is meagre fare indeed.

> I. LORD. What time o' day is 't, Apemantus?
> APEMANTUS. Time to be honest.
> I. LORD. That time serves still.
> APEMANTUS. The more accursèd thou that still omit'st it.
> (I. i. 254–57)

Such dismal exchanges as this reveal the hopelessly ambivalent basis

[15] Kenneth Burke *"Timon of Athens* and Misanthropic Gold," contained in *Language as Symbolic Action: Essays on Life, Literature, and Method* (Berkeley: Univ. of California Press, 1966), p. 117.

of Apemantus' verbal behavior. He is compelled to use language as his means to deny communication, just as he must be present at Timon's communal banquet in order to give force to his churlish gesture of defiance.

> TIMON. O, Apemantus, you are welcome.
> APEMANTUS.   No,
> You shall not make me welcome;
> I come to have thee thrust me out of doors.
> (I. ii. 23–25)

The sterile atomism of Athenian society appears most clearly in Apemantus' use of language. He does not use words as a medium to promote mutual enrichment between congenial beings but rather as an arsenal of blunt weapons to supply a constant battle for transcendence. Hence, his conversations with others have a jerky, non-sequential, seesaw rhythm, as the combatants paratactically take up the various topics brought forth for battle and hurl them briefly back and forth. The resulting linguistic configuration does not have a progressive dimension at all: no organic interdependence of parts within a whole. Instead, the verbal patterns are static, spatial, and lifeless. For instance, the disjunct, stichomythic nature of the one hundred lines of dialogue that follows Apemantus' initial appearance (I. i. 170–270) issues in no sense of continuity nor reveals any growth of knowledge; it simply permits the exfoliation of a set pattern of verbal insult. Apemantus' exchange with Timon's creditors (II. ii. 46–120) also merely repeats this directionless pattern of talk.

The oddities of Apemantus' speech are important because they prefigure the essential shape of Timon's own experience with language in the second half of the play. The massive invective Timon launches against all existence is mostly fueled by a seemingly inexhaustible parade of visitors who figure forth themes rich with possibilities for great verbal amplification: war, prostitution, money, and thievery. Like the various motifs offered to Apemantus to fire his talent for insult those unsolicited visitor-topics approach Timon's cave in paratactic sequence, stay until their verbal charge has been exhausted, and then disappear, except Alcibiades, from the play forever. No causal logic controls the order of their appearance, and, as E. A. J. Honigmann notes, they neither interact nor stand in any sort of meaningful relationship to each other.[16] Even within the relatively brief span of a

[16] E. A. J. Honigmann, *"Timon of Athens," Shakespeare Quarterly*, 12 (1961), p. 17.

diatribe on a single topic there is really no sense of an organic and continuous development of thought. In fact, we may recognize in Timon's long utterances the same broken rhythms and fractured sequences of Apemantus' discourse, only now magnified greatly. Timon's outbursts habitually consist of rather loosely connected exclamations, which tend to string together an assortment of maledictions and yearnings, disjointed thoughts and images, until the coruscating blaze of his anger is momentarily interrupted and then redirected by the timely arrival of yet another visitor.[17] Those similarities should remind us that the language of the play is part of the closed system of disjunct relationships binding Timon and Apemantus both to each other and to their societies. Just as those characters can only rearrange themselves into discrete patterns that reveal, from different vantage points, the same old hopeless relationship, so too Timon's diatribes can finally only express multiple revelations of what is essentially the same unchanging predicament. In *Timon of Athens* there is only one escape from the constraints of a false social language, and that is the one Timon gradually moves towards and finally accepts with full understanding of its ontological implications. "Lips, let sour words go by and language end" (v. i. 218).

IV

Timon's radical experience with "sour words" requires close attention, since the manner in which he first exploits and then abandons language bears directly on Shakespeare's own attitude towards his medium during this experimental period. Fleeing from all contact with humanity Timon declares "Nothing I'll bear from thee / But nakedness, thou detestable town" (IV. i. 32–33), and he proceeds to strip himself, Lear-fashion, of all the social attributes that mediate between him and the demonic reality he has glimpsed in Athenian ingratitude. Since language is inextricably linked to the hated social order, it is not surprising that it receives the brunt of his attack. "Breath infect breath," he cries, "That their society, as their friendship, may / Be merely poison!" (30–32). Still, as we saw previously, Timon remains subject to the confining nature of Athenian discourse. Unable to surrender it forthrightly, he retains language but attempts to transform it from its discredited function as a medium for fruitful social intercourse into an instrument for the immediate articulation of a personally envisioned

[17] W. H. Clemen, *The Development of Shakespeare's Imagery* (London: Methuen, 1951), p. 171.

truth. With this attempt a chasm of great generic consequence opens in the topography of *Timon of Athens*: a schism with implications for poetic drama that Shakespeare cannot ignore.

By taking sovereign possession of language Timon empowers his words with the ability to create a world that is vastly richer and more complex than the impoverished Athenian milieu of the first three acts. However, this rich world of Timon's imagination emerges in sharp contrast to the real world of his actual former experience, and its reality suffers a corresponding attenuation. "Madmen have such seething brains." another Athenian reminds us, "Such shaping fantasies . . ." (*MND*. V. i. 4–5), and this is especially true of Timon in his misan-throphy. The thrust of his general denunciations is severely blunted by a widening disjunction between the magnificently stratified and varie-gated society he pictures in his curses and the diminished and polarized culture he has recently abandoned. For instance, Timon's curse that "Matrons, turn incontinent! / Obedience fail in children! . . . To general filths / Convert o' th' instant, green virginity!" (IV. i. 3–7) does not so much terrify as remind us of all that was missing from the womanless, childless Athens we left with Timon. Timon's bloody instructions to Alcibiades to disregard the "yells of mothers, maids, [and] babes" (IV. iii. 125) in his planned assault on Athens strikes a similarly hollow note. Paradoxically, it is only when Timon has com-pletely repudiated all forms of social mediation that his words begin to give us a picture of what mediated existence really looks like with all its various institutions, occupations, and religious traditions. His wide-ranging diatribes now encompass

> Piety and fear,
> Religion to the gods, peace, justice, truth,
> Domestic awe, night-rest and neighborhood,
> Instruction, manners, mysteries and trades,
> Degrees, observances, customs and laws, . . .
> (IV. i. 15-19)

Such passages make no direct contact with the carefully delimited world of the play's first three acts. Instead, they carry us away from that play into another world characterized by the crowded mediacy of actual human existence: a world that exists more as the shadowy creation of Timon's increasingly solipsistic imagination than as a dramatic reality. Language, it begins to appear, has been simultaneously liberated and invalidated.

The rigidly dialectical structure of the first half of *Timon of*

Athens did not allow Timon much occasion for eloquence. When he leaves the narrow confines of the walled city, he imagines himself released from the linguistic constraints of that culture into a more spacious area of verbal possibilities. The vague unlocalized nature of the new space Timon now inhabits does suggest that the trajectory of his flight from society has a generic as well as a geographic dimension. He appears to have moved from a structure whose radical of presentation is dramatic to one whose mode of address is essentially lyric and satiric. Somewhat like the Forest of Arden, where exiles find "tongues in trees, books in running brooks, / Sermons in stones" (*AYLI*. II. i. 16–17), the wilderness offers Timon an unlimited range of self-expression. Put in this context, we can see that the misanthrope's abandonment of society would have a certain appeal to Shakespeare since it would provide him, as Kenneth Burke suggests, with "the pretext for as intense and far-ranging an exercise in invective as the poet was capable of."[18] But this sphere of total free speech and unmediated self-expression, whatever the obvious short-range attractions, is finally hopelessly sterile for both poet and misanthrope. Neither can live long in its limitless expanse.

Timon soon learns that the very fact of a completely personal possession of language becomes the measure of its uselessness. His tremendous execrations exhaust his power but actually make little effect on the society he has abandoned. They discount his speech ahead of time on the reasonable basis of his self-disenfranchisement. "Who can speak broader than he that has no house to put his head in? Such may rail against great buildings" (III. iv. 63–65). The uncircumscribed utterances of Timon's rage (despite their purely linguistic magnificence) have very little effective social and dramatic impact but tend to spill out into the limitless void created by his disengagement from society. The dreadful imprecations hang before us in all their fiery brightness for a brief time and then float away into the boundless space surrounding the speaker, leaving not a rack behind to disturb our distanced contemplation of his dilemma. Lacking the discipline of boundaries, Timon's imagination soars upward into rather ludicrous speculations about cosmic thievery (e.g., "the sun's a thief"). Hence, Timon and his language become increasingly disembodied once they are freed from the corporeality of social interdependence. As Shakespeare surely recognizes, the problem is that words lose their substance and, more seriously, cease even to have dimensions of truth and

[18] Burke, p. 115.

falsehood once they have been severed from their mediating functions in social intercourse. In the light of that knowledge, Timon can express a total disregard for the degree of truth or falsehood contained in speech when he greets the Senators who visit him in Act V.

> Speak and be hanged!
> For each true word a blister, and each false
> Be as a cauterizing to the root o' th' tongue,
> Consuming it with speaking!
> (V. i. 129–32)

Timon's death is imminent in this attitude towards language. Indeed, the last phrase is an excellent summation of his paradoxical experience with free speech in Acts IV and V of the play. For if that experience has liberated him into a new, less restricted form of being, it has also gradually destroyed him as a dramatic presence. Timon's personal transcendence ends in linguistic suicide: he consumes himself with speaking.

V

The exact nature of Timon's death is unclear, for unlike the suicides of Brutus, Othello, and Antony, his demise is neither dramatized nor described in any detail.[19] This vagueness disperses, however, when we recognize how exclusively verbal Timon's identity has become by the end of the play. For Timon, to cease speaking is to cease to be, and in his final address to the world—"Lips, let sour words go by and language end"—he unequivocally acquiesces in this form of self-annihilation: "Timon hath done his reign" (V. i. 218–21). Throughout the latter part of the play, in fact, Timon is obsessed with hostile actions directed against others that eventually rebound upon the aggressor: a motif of clear relevance to his own self-destructive misanthropy and verbal belligerence. "There's gold to pay thy soldiers," Timon tells Alcibiades as he urges him on against Athens; "Make large confusion; and, thy fury spent, / Confounded be thyself!" (IV. iii. 127–29). "The gods confound them all in thy conquest," he says, "And thee after, when thou hast conquerèd!" (104–05). Turning to the two whores who accompany Alcibiades, Timon gives them gold and, in the same ironic vein, urges them to use their syphilitic bodies first to destroy lecherous mankind and then themselves.

[19] Honigmann says, "Timon's suicide is hinted at but not definitely asserted," (p. 17).

>   Plague all,
> That your activity may defeat and quell
> The source of all erection. There's more gold.
> Do you damn others and let this damn you,
> And ditches grave you all!
>   (IV. iii. 162–66)

Speaking to Apemantus, Timon pictures the whole of life as a vicious closed system in which all forms of being are destroyed by their own destructive impulses. "Wert thou the unicorn," he says, "pride and wrath would confound thee and make thine own self the conquest of thy fury" (IV. iii. 333–35). The unicorn image may have special bearing on Timon's own self-defeating narcissism. After preaching on the topic of universal destructiveness, he dispatches the Banditti to Athens with the by now familiar instructions: "To Athens go; / Break open shops; ... / Steal less for this I give you, / And gold confound you howsoe'er!" (IV. iii. 442–45). Timon next riddlingly instructs the Poet and Painter to so deploy their murderous instincts that they will inadvertently destroy each other (V. i. 84–106). His fixation on self-consuming activities finally concludes with his ironic invitation to the Athenians to end the misery of existence by hanging themselves from his tree (V. i. 203–10). To Timon the universe seems increasingly to be a place in which only self-destructive acts are possible. Suicide, either direct or indirect, becomes the rule of all life, including his own.

By emphasizing the self-consuming nature of hostile actions, Shakespeare fashions a context within which we can understand Timon's own inexorable movement towards self-extinction. More importantly, however, Shakespeare uses this context to alert us to his own awareness of what he as an artist has been doing and of the dangers he foresees in his course. In his monomaniac actions and language Timon has been slowly destroying himself as a dramatic entity by attacking the very structure that sustains his being. Shakespeare's apparent willingness to attend the misanthrope on his drift towards nonbeing suggests his own temporary commitment to a concomitant aesthetic suicide. He appears to have designed a play licensed to pursue its own generic collapse by a perverse rejection of its own medium. But the impression grows that Shakespeare's control and scrutiny of Timon's suicidal behavior are simultaneously meditations on his own involvement with poetic drama, since both artist and protagonist seem engaged in a revolt against the constraints of mediation. Hence, one of Timon's last acts is to cynically reject the worth of the Poet's craft. "I am rapt," the visiting

Poet hypocritically admits, "and cannot cover / The monstrous bulk of this ingratitude / With any size of words." "Let it go naked," is Timon's rejoinder; "men may see't the better" (V. i. 62–65). Such exchanges reveal how Shakespeare can both identify with and distance himself from the problems raised in his play-world. For do we not hear in the Poet's remark Shakespeare's own confession of a general linguistic inadequacy in the "monstrous bulk" of words with which he has supplied Timon? Whatever the answer, we surely do recognize in Timon's blunt response the passion for immediacy that both he and his creator share. Having experienced the deadly consequences of that passion, the two men can finally part company. Timon succumbs to suicidal silence, but Shakespeare goes on to finish the play in a new key.

Shakespeare has accompanied Timon in his withdrawal from mediacy just about as far as the dramatic artist dares to go—indeed perhaps too far. In his full misanthropy Timon becomes a brutally "end-of-the-line character," [20] and as such he represents a dangerous point of no return for the dramatist. Everything about the condition of immediacy Timon achieves turns out to be paradoxical and self-consuming: his drive towards full autonomy is consummated in nothingness, and his usurpation of language terminates in silence. Although Timon's cry of "nothing brings me all things" (V. i. 186) may truly summarize his final attainment of transcendence from a constricting medium, for the creative artist—who may understandably long for such liberation—it must forever remain an unrealizable goal. "The immediate is not for him," Sigurd Burckhardt says of the poet, "his office is to shape through the most mediate of media." [21] The impetus that propels the play forward after Timon's death arises from Shakespeare's final acknowledgment of the constraints imposed on all human activities by our inherent subjection to between-ness and continuity. His usefulness to Shakespeare now exhausted, Timon can be released into the "everlasting mansion" on the shores of the sterile "salt flood" (V. i. 213–14) with full understanding of Apemantus' earlier analysis: "The middle of humanity thou never knewest" (IV. iii. 299). It is to the abandoned world of mediation, the carefully excluded "middle of humanity," that Shakespeare now returns in the concluding scene of *Timon of Athens*.

Shakespeare's abrupt transition from Timon's last death-directed gestures to the crowded urban scenes that end the play has seemed to many critics the most jarring disjunction in "this drama of

[20] Burke, p. 118.
[21] Burckhardt, pp. 278–279.

the gaps." [22] The debate and ensuing reconciliation between Alcibiades and the Athenian Senators appear to belong to an entirely different world. The logic behind the shift of focus becomes visible, however, when we consider the kind of fundamental reorganization of the play that is taking place in these scenes. The besieged Senators appear to Alcibiades for mercy by calling attention to the great difference between the Athens that forced him and Timon into banishment and the present Athens.

> These walls of ours
> Were not erected by their hands from whom
> You have received your griefs: nor are they such
> That these great tow'rs, trophies, and schools should fall
> For private faults in them.
> (V. iv. 22–26)

This is not the impoverished city of the play's first half. The reference to "these great tow'rs, trophies, and schools" reminds us of those various social institutions that normally mediate between individual and community: agencies of concord notably absent from the former Athens. Emphasis now falls, for the first time, on process and historical continuity, and in this new temporal context the Senators can argue convincingly that "all have not offended. . . . / Crimes like lands, / Are not inherited" (35–38). Based on the humane virtues of moderation and compromise, that reasonable plea persuades Alcibiades to "Approach the fold and cull th' infected forth, / But kill not all together" (43–44).

Unlike Timon, Alcibiades has no quarrel with society per se but only with a particular social disease within an otherwise healthy social organism. His hostile attack on Athens, although it does threaten the physical well-being of the city, does not strike at the essential ethical basis of communal life. Indeed, his rebellious posture may be reasonably construed as socially therapeutic and even patriotic, since he is attempting to recall his degenerate society back to its neglected ideals and to get

---

[22] Northrop Frye finds that "Timon is oddly isolated from the final action, in which the breach between Alcibiades and the Athenians closes up over his head, in striking contrast with conclusions of most of the other tragedies, where nobody is allowed to steal the show from the central character." *Anatomy of Criticism: Four Essays* (Princeton: Princeton Univ. Press, 1957), p. 221. To Ellis-Fermor, *Timon's* last act "is so erratic in the relating of its parts that we sometimes feel as if we are reading a mixture of two different plays" (p. 280). G. B. Harrison charges that the fifth act "is little more than disjointed fragments." *Shakespeare's Tragedies* (London: Routledge and Kegan Paul, 1951), p. 267.

it to function again in its customary manner. As he accepts his new responsibilities in a reformed Athens he underscores the social values of "regular justice" and "public laws."

> Not a man
> Shall pass his quarter or offend the stream
> Of regular justice in your city's bounds
> But shall be rendered to your public laws
> At heaviest answer.
> (V. iv. 59–63).

Timon's absolutism threatened to carry the play beyond the limits of possible communal existence, but now Alcibiades re-establishes the bounds of social behavior and community. The image of "the stream / Of regular justice" suggests cultural continuity and the normal cycles of social life. But the strongest indication of renewed mediation in the emergent Athenian society occurs in the last four lines of the play. "Bring me into your city," Alcibiades says,

> And I will use the olive with my sword,
> Make war breed peace, make peace stint war, make each
> Prescribe to other, as each other's leech.
> (V. iv. 81–84)

Disturbing memories of Timon's bitter abdication may remain, but the play leaves us firmly in the midst of human interdependence.

The play ends as Athens opens her gates to receive her redeemer. Perhaps it is not too fanciful to glimpse in that spectacle Shakespeare's own reconciliation with a medium of which he had grown distrustful. The Senators' attempt to speak with Timon ("Timon! Timon! / Look out, and speak to friends" [V. i. 125–26]) was answered with a curse that all language end. But the Senators' eloquent appeal to Alcibiades leads to understanding and a strengthening of the social bond. " 'Tis most nobly spoken," they say of Alcibiades' agreement, and he answers, "Descend, and keep your words" (62–63). Language has made a new union possible. In this regard Shakespeare's abrupt shift from Timon to Alcibiades—from an unmediated to a mediated sense of existence—may have metadramatic significance as well as mimetic. It suggests how a great artist works to understand and come to terms with the inherent requirements of his art. To see *Timon of Athens* in this light is to strengthen its value, since it marks a climactic juncture in Shakespeare's restless exploration into his demanding medium.

Conclusion

This book has arisen out of a desire to celebrate. But what is the proper praise of Shakespeare? It is not uncommon for lovers of language and expression to speak of his work as having defined and exhausted the limits of linguistic possibility. We marvel at the unparalleled breadth of his working vocabulary, the vivid immediacy of his utterance, and the easy familiarity with which he surveys and names the human scene. He seems to us the most generous and expansive of poets in that, under his liberating care, words and phrases are never "cabined, cribbed, confined," but always encouraged to realize the full potential of their inherent meanings. "More than any other human intellect of which we have adequate record," George Steiner says, "Shakespeare used language in a condition of total possibility."[1] "To read Shakespeare," he explains,

> is to be in contact with a verbal medium of unequaled richness and exactitude; with a mode of statement which does not, as in ordinary men, limit itself to a conventional, fixed pattern of significance, but persistently conveys a multiple, creative energy of thought and feeling. We speak as if words were a piano score; Shakespeare's is full orchestration.[2]

[1] George Steiner, *Language and Silence: Essays on Language, Literature and the Inhuman* (New York: Atheneum, 1967), p. 206.
[2] Ibid., p. 207.

Shakespeare's astonishing creative empathy—his "negative capability"—extends not only to his characters but to language itself, endowing both with the freedom to display their essential complexity and plenitude. He seems to find in the medium of poetic drama a capacity and amplitude fully answerable to the vast polyphonic structure of the universe surrounding him. Indeed, the expressive order merely complements the phenomenal. No wonder we, as critics, must strain to describe the inclusive scope of his vision. "Shakespeare's dramatic economy is prodigally lavish," Erich Auerbach remarks; "it bears witness to his delight in rendering the most varied phenomena of life, and this delight in turn is inspired by the concept that the cosmos is everywhere interdependent, so that every chord of human destiny arouses a multitude of voices to parallel or contrary motion."[3] We turn almost instinctively to musical metaphors ("full orchestration," "polyphonic structure," "every chord of human destiny") in order to suggest the complex harmonies of his idiom and the range of his accomplishment. Impatient of all constraints Shakespeare glances "from heaven to earth, from earth to heaven" and articulates his perception in a verbal medium of sufficient magnitude. Steiner says he "appears to have been the last to enclose in poetic speech a total view of human action, a *summa mundi*."[4] Here was a poet! When comes such another?

No significant departure from this estimate of Shakespeare is likely to command much assent. Still, we should recognize how our enthusiasm can paradoxically diminish his actual achievement. The appreciative remarks of Steiner and Auerbach, for example, suggest rather misleadingly that Shakespeare enjoyed full mastery over a dramatic medium capable of holding the mirror up to nature and that he was indeed able to show the very age and body of his time its form and pressure. Although it is not their intent, those writers invite us to see Shakespeare as the fortunate artist—so lovingly recalled by the *Folio* editors—whose "mind and hand went together," whose every creative thought was "uttered with that uneasiness, that we scarce received from him a blot in his papers." No doubt a large part of Shakespeare's genius corresponds to that description, but to endorse it completely is to neglect the more interesting poet who pursues a difficult, ongoing struggle for a satisfactory relation with his craft. What happens, for instance, to that vital figure of the Sonnets who can both exult in his "pow'rful rime" (55) and suffer "The barren tender of a poet's debt"(83)? Instead of a

[3] Erich Auerbach, *Mimesis: The Representation of Reality in Western Literature,* trans. Willard R. Trask (Princeton: Princeton Univ. Press, 1953), p. 323.
[4] Steiner, p. 205.

poet laboring to release his "tongue-tied Muse(85)," we can inadvertently pay homage to an artist so totally in control of his subservient medium that no real possibility of any meaningful encounter appears conceivable between him and his materials. Unless we stay alert to poetic realities we can picture a demiurge in place of the mere mortal who, in Sonnet III, laments that "my nature is subdued / To what it works in, like the dyer's hand."

I have tried to show some of the ways in which the well-intentioned traditional view of Shakespeare's artistry needs to be qualified by a more dynamic sense of his ceaseless engagement with his medium's expressive potential. My emphasis has fallen on an artist quite aware of the degree to which his nature is subdued to the medium in which it works, and on his willingness to make that debilitating subjection a leading theme in certain plays. Communication—both verbal and nonverbal—is a central and conscious issue in the plays I have examined, not only for the characters but for the playwright himself. Neither word nor act is finally adequate to the aspirations of those characters: speech often hinders rather than fulfills communication; action retards the completion of intended design, and mediators accidently cheapen and pervert the unions they work to establish. It seems that Shakespeare is projecting into both the content and structure of the plays his sensitivity to the divisive and obstructive forces latent in his medium. Like other great innovative writers, he cannot help but express his knowledge that language, at times, can be experienced as a frustrating limitation: it can encumber and adulterate the artist's intentions as well as realize them. His sensitivity extends not only to his "rough and all-unable pen," but also to the limitations arising from his felt bondage to "the flat unraisèd spirits" of his actors and the "unworthy scaffold" of his stage. His situation vis-à-vis his audience can, on occasion, appear equally disheartening. He knows, to quote again from *Henry V*, that we have no recourse but to "sit and see, / Minding true things by what their mock'ries be" (IV. Cho. 52–53). Beside the omnipotent word master serenely indulging his linguistic and dramatic adequacy I have tried to place a different but equally recognizable figure: a creator who in his frustrated desire to transcend the limiting mediacy of his art can cry out for "a Muse of fire, that would ascend / The brightest heaven of invention" (Prol. 1–4). This, too, is an aspect of Shakespeare we can understand and celebrate.

Is there not something grand, something of tragic stature, in the dynamic image of the man who can invoke a "Muse of fire"? The poet himself seems to recapitulate the experience of his most heroic characters: he chafes against the mediated nature of art-making even as he is forced to acknowledge his inescapable subjection to it. Like his overweening tragic protagonists, dreaming of immediacy and transcendence, he too would "crown [his] thoughts with acts, be it thought and done" (*Mac.* IV. i. 149). If possible, he would be "all in all sufficient" (*Oth.* IV. i. 258); he would be "the King himself" (*Lear.* IV. vi. 84) whose coinings we dare not touch. In his drive for artistic integrity, he would refuse all compromise and flattery and "stand / As if a man were author of himself / And knew no other kin" (*Cor.* V. iii. 35–37). The magnitude of those heroic figures reflects back upon their maker, so that we observe the degree to which he shares with his protagonists a desire for an immediacy of creative expression. His will towards "solely sovereign sway and masterdom" (*Mac.* I. v. 68) over his medium is their will also. However, the dramatic contexts from which those several statements arise reveal Shakespeare's clear awareness that such aspirations will finally be dashed by tragic inevitability. The wish to "suit the action to the word, the word to the action" (*Ham.* III. ii. 16–17) is passionately voiced but never fully consummated within the varied worlds of Shakespearean tragedy. His characters must either follow Alcibiades and acquiesce in the mediated constitution of the human condition, or follow Timon and lapse into silence and death. By projecting over-reachers like Othello and Lear, Coriolanus and Timon, Shakespeare is able vicariously to experience and come to terms with those alternatives. It follows that Shakespeare's relation to his medium is not static and untroubled, but profoundly complex and, at times, potentially tragic in its gradual evolution.

Finally we must attempt to achieve a balanced perspective. In my reaction to some excesses of bardolatry I have not wished to encourage an equally misleading view of Shakespeare. If he is not a complacent demiurge, neither is he a modern artist carrying an almost intolerable burden of self-consciousness about his anguished predicament. Language is a pressing concern, but it has not yet become for him, as Susan Sontag says it has for many contemporary writers, "the most impure, the most contaminated, the most exhausted of all materials out of which art is made." [5] In fact, the bulk of his work conveys the opposite impression. Nevertheless, there are striking instances (I think particularly of *Troilus* and *Timon*) when Shakespeare's attitude towards his seemingly hostile medium comes near to the modern sense of radical disenchantment. During such recurrent moments, Sontag's description

[5] Susan Sontag, *Styles of Radical Will* (New York: Dell, Delta Books, 1970), p. 14.

of what she believes is a relatively new kind of artistic *malaise* may have a special relevance.

> The "spirit" seeking embodiment in art clashes with the "material" character of art itself. Art is unmasked as gratuitous, and the very concreteness of the artist's tools (and, particularly in the case of language, their historicity) appears as a trap. Practiced in a world furnished with second-hand perceptions, and especially confounded by the treachery of words, the artist's activity is cursed with mediacy. Art becomes the enemy of the artist, for it denies him the realization—the transcendence—he desires.[6]

The man who wrote *Measure for Measure* would have no trouble understanding how the materiality of language can effectively corrupt spiritual longings. Indeed the motif appears prominently in *Romeo and Juliet* and several other plays. Nor would "the treachery of words" seem an odd concept to him. Moreover, Shakespeare knows full well, as he puts it in Sonnet 76, that "all my best is dressing old words new, / Speaking again what is already spent." A particularly urgent problem in *Troilus and Cressida* concerns the historicity of language in that neither lover nor warrior seems able to find, from the available stylistic storehouse, the idiom appropriate to his behavior. There are even occasions, as we have seen, when Shakespeare explores dramatically the degree to which the artist may feel that his activity is "cursed with mediacy"—instances when his ongoing critique of art-making begins to assume the curious form of "anti-art."[7] (One reason *Troilus, Measure,* and *Timon* resist clear general classification is probably because such anti-formal impulses are operative during their creation.) Even so, a crucial difference remains between Shakespeare and the artist Sontag describes. The peculiar plays I have selected for study are best seen as temporary and experimental probes into the mediated character of play-making, rather than as Shakespeare's settled conviction. In his restless search for understanding he eventually surveys the full spectrum of possible responses to the problem of mediacy, but he never rests long in

---

[6] Ibid., p. 5.

[7] The notion of "anti-art" in Shakespeare is not as eccentric as one might think. Philip Edwards, a long-established Shakespearean scholar, says *Troilus and Cressida* "seems somehow 'anti-art' or 'pre-art' in its refusal of a coherent form which might work against the picture of incoherence which is the matter of the play." *Shakespeare and the Confines of Art* (London: Methuen, 1968), p. 107.

a place where art can become "the enemy of the artist." At his most triumphant moments—in *King Lear,* for instance—he manages to portray his art as both treacherous and insubstantial and as our least indispensable possession. The scrutiny is radical, but the faith holds firm.

My object has been to praise Shakespeare, but the very plays I have chosen remind me how risky such an undertaking can be. Pandarus' efforts to extol Troilus only draw from Cressida the rejoinder that "more in Troilus thousandfold I see / Than in the glass of Pandar's praise may be" (I. ii. 270–71). Can we as celebrants of Shakespeare hope for a much better ratio of praise to perception? Between the critical enterprise and the pandar's trade there may not be a very great difference. This melancholy identification suggests that criticism itself participates unwittingly in the processes of tragic mediation I have been tracing: not a happy thought, certainly, but one perhaps sufficiently contrite to conclude this study.

Bibliography

ALEXANDER, PETER. *Shakespeare's Life and Art.* London: James Nisbet, 1939.

ALPERS, PAUL J. *"King Lear* and the Theory of the Sight Pattern." *In Defense of Reading.* Ed. R. Brower and R. Poirier. New York: Dutton, 1963, 133–52.

ARISTOTLE. *The Poetics.* Trans. S. H. Butcher. London: Macmillan, 1911.

ARNHEIM, RUDOLF. *Art and Visual Perception: A Psychology of the Creative Eye.* Berkeley: Univ. of California Press, 1954.

AUERBACH, ERICH. *Mimesis: The Representation of Reality in Western Literature.* Trans. Willard R. Trask. Princeton: Princeton Univ. Press, 1953.

BARBER, C. L. *Shakespeare's Festive Comedy: A Study of Dramatic Form and its Relation to Social Custom.* Princeton: Princeton Univ. Press, 1959.

BATTENHOUSE, ROY W. *"Measure for Measure* and Christian Doctrine of Atonement." PMLA, 61 (1946), 1029–59.

BENNETT, JOSEPHINE W. *"Measure for Measure" as Royal Entertainment.* New York: Columbia Univ. Press, 1966.

BERGER, HARRY JR. *"Troilus and Cressida*: the Observer as Basilisk." *Comparative Drama,* 6 (1968–69), 22–36.

BETHELL, S. L. *Shakespeare and the Popular Dramatic Tradition.* London: Staples Press, 1944.

BLAU, HERBERT. "A Subtext Based on Nothing." *Tulane Drama Review,* 8 (1963), 125.

149

BOOTH, STEPHEN. "On the Value of *Hamlet.*" *Reinterpretations of Elizabethan Drama.* Ed. Norman Rabkin. New York: Columbia Univ. Press, 1969.

BOOTH, WAYNE. *The Rhetoric of Fiction.* Chicago: Univ. of Chicago Press, 1961.

BRADBROOK, M. C. "Authority, Truth, and Justice in *Measure for Measure.*" MLR, 41 (1946), 246–55.

———. *The Tragic Pageant of "Timon of Athens."* Cambridge: Cambridge Univ. Press, 1966.

BRADLEY, A. C. *Shakespearean Tragedy: Lectures on "Hamlet," "Othello," "King Lear," "Macbeth."* 1904 rpt. London: Macmillan, 1967.

BRIEN, ALAN. "Openings: London." *Theatre Arts,* 47 (1963), 58–59.

BROOKE, NICHOLAS. "The Ending of *King Lear.*" *Shakespeare 1564–1964.* Ed. E. A. Bloom. Providence, R. I.: Brown Univ. Press, 1964.

———. *Shakespeare's Early Tragedies.* London: Methuen, 1968.

———. *"King Lear."* Studies in English Literature, no. 15. London: Edward Arnold, 1963.

BROOKE, TUCKER. *Essays on Shakespeare.* London: Methuen, 1948.

BROWER, REUBEN. *Hero and Saint: Shakespeare and the Graeco-Roman Heroic Tradition.* Oxford: Oxford Univ. Press, 1971.

BRYANT, J. A. JR. *Hippolyta's View: Some Christian Aspects of Shakespeare's Plays.* Lexington, Ky.: Univ. of Kentucky Press, 1961.

BULAND, MABLE. *The Presentation of Time in the Elizabethan Drama.* Yale Studies in English, 44. New York, 1912.

BULLOUGH, GEOFFREY. *Narrative and Dramatic Sources of Shakespeare,* vols. 1–7. New York: Columbia Univ. Press, 1957–73.

BURCKHARDT, SIGURD. *Shakespearean Meanings.* Princeton: Princeton Univ. Press, 1968.

BURKE, KENNETH. "*Timon of Athens* and Misanthropic Gold." *Language as Symbolic Action: Essays on Life, Literature, and Method.* Berkeley: Univ. of California Press, 1966.

CALDERWOOD, JAMES L. *Shakespearean Metadrama.* Minneapolis, Minn.: Univ. of Minnesota Press, 1971.

CAMPBELL, O. J. *Comicall Satyre and Shakespeare's "Troilus and Cressida."* San Marino, Calif.: The Huntington Library, 1938.

———. *Shakespeare's Satire.* New York: Oxford Univ. Press, 1943.

CASSIRER, ERNST. *Language and Myth.* Trans. Susanne K. Langer. New York: Dover, 1953.

CAVELL, STANLEY. *Must We Mean What We Say?: Modern Philosophical Essays in Morality, Religion, Drama, Music, and Criticism.* New York: Scribner's, 1969.

CHAMBERS, E. K. *William Shakespeare: A Study of Facts and Problems.* 2 vols. Oxford: Oxford Univ. Press, 1930.

CHAMBERS, R. W. *"King Lear." Glasgow University Publications,* 59 (1940), 20–52.

CHANG, JOSEPH S. M. J. "The Language of Paradox in *Romeo and Juliet." Shakespeare Studies,* 3 (1967), 22–42.

CLEMEN, W. H. *The Development of Shakespeare's Imagery.* London: Methuen, 1951.

COGHILL, NEVILL. "Comic Form in *Measure for Measure." Shakespeare Survey,* 8 (1955), 14–26.

COLE, DOUGLAS. "Introduction." *Twentieth Century Interpretations of "Romeo and Juliet."* Englewood Cliffs, N. J.: Prentice-Hall, 1970.

COLERIDGE, S. T. *Shakespearean Criticism.* Ed. T. M. Raysor, 2 vols. London: Dent, Everyman Library edition, 1960.

COLLINS, A. S. *"Timon of Athens:* A Reconsideration." RES, 22 (1946), 96–108.

COOK, DAVID. *"Timon of Athens." Shakespeare Survey,* 16 (1963), 83–95.

CRAIG, HARDIN. *An Interpretation of Shakespeare.* New York: Columbia Univ. Press, 1948.

CUNNINGHAM, J. V. *Woe or Wonder: The Emotional Effect of Shakespearean Tragedy.* Denver, Colo.: Alan Swallow, 1951.

CURTIUS, E. R. *European Literature and the Latin Middle Ages.* Trans. Willard R. Trask. New York: Pantheon Books, 1953.

DANBY, JOHN F. *Poets on Fortune's Hill: Studies in Sidney, Shakespeare, Beaumont and Fletcher.* London: Faber and Faber, 1952.
———. *Shakespeare's Doctrine of Nature: A Study of "King Lear."* London: Faber and Faber, 1949.

DE MAN, PAUL. *Blindness and Insight: Essays in the Rhetoric of Contemporary Criticism.* Oxford: Oxford Univ. Press, 1971.

DORAN, MADELEINE. *Endeavors of Art: A Study of Form in Elizabethan Drama.* Madison, Wis.: Univ. of Wisconsin Press, 1954.

DRAPER, J. W. "The Theme of *Timon of Athens." MLR,* 29 (1934), 20–31.

DRIVER, TOM F. *The Sense of History in Greek and Shakespearean Drama.* New York: Columbia Univ. Press, 1960.

EAGLETON, TERENCE. *Shakespeare and Society: Critical Studies in Shakespearean Drama.* New York: Schocken Books, 1967.

EDWARDS, PHILIP. *Shakespeare and the Confines of Art.* London: Methuen, 1968.

ELIOT, T. S. *Selected Essays.* New York: Harcourt, Brace, 1932.

ELLIS-FERMOR, UNA. *The Frontiers of Drama.* London: Methuen, 1946.
———. *Shakespeare the Dramatist, and other papers.* London: Methuen, 1961.

ELTON, WILLIAM R. *"King Lear" and the Gods.* San Marino, Calif.: The Huntington Library, 1966.

———. "Shakespeare's Ulysses and the Problem of Value." *Shakespeare Studies* 2 (1966), 95–111.

EMPSON, WILLIAM. *Some Versions of Pastoral.* London: Chatto & Windus, 1935.

———. *The Structure of Complex Words.* London: Chatto & Windus, 1951

EVANS, BERTRAND. *Shakespeare's Comedies.* Oxford: Oxford Univ. Press, 1960.

FARNHAM, WILLARD. *Shakespeare's Tragic Frontier: The World of His Final Tragedies.* Berkeley: Univ. of California Press, 1950.

FERGUSSON, FRANCIS. *The Idea of a Theater: A Study of Ten Plays. The Art of Drama in Changing Perspective.* Princeton: Princeton Univ. Press, 1949.

———. "*Macbeth* as the Imitation of an Action." *English Institute Essays, 1951.* New York: Columbia Univ. Press, 1952.

FLETCHER, ANGUS. *Allegory: The Theory of a Symbolic Mode.* Ithaca, N. Y.: Cornell Univ. Press, 1964.

FLUCHÈRE, HENRI. *Shakespeare and the Elizabethans.* Trans. Guy Hamilton. New York: Hill and Wang, 1956.

FRASER, RUSSELL A. *Shakespeare's Poetics in Relation to "King Lear."* London: Routledge and Kegan Paul, 1962.

FROST, WILLIAM. "Shakespeare's Rituals and the Opening of *King Lear.*" *Hudson Review,* 10 (1958), 577–85.

FRYE, DEAN. "The Question of Shakespearean 'Parody.'" EIC, 15 (1965), 19–33.

FRYE, NORTHROP. *A Natural Perspective: The Development of Shakespearean Comedy and Romance.* New York: Columbia Univ. Press, 1965.

———. *Anatomy of Criticism: Four Essays.* Princeton: Princeton Univ. Press, 1957.

———. *Fools of Time: Studies in Shakespearean Tragedy.* Toronto: Univ. of Toronto Press, 1967.

GODDARD. HAROLD C. *The Meaning of Shakespeare.* 2 vols. Chicago: Univ. of Chicago Press, 1951.

GOMBRICH, E. H. *Art and Illusion: A Study in the Psychology of Pictorial Representation.* New York: Pantheon Books, Bollinger Series, 1960.

———. *The Story of Art.* London: Phaidon Paperback, 1950.

GOODMAN, PAUL. *The Structure of Literature.* Chicago: Univ. of Chicago Press, 1954.

GORDON, D. J. "Name and Fame; Shakespeare's *Coriolanus.*" *Papers Mainly Shakespearian.* Ed. G. I. Duthie. Aberdeen University Studies, no. 147. Edinburgh: Oliver and Boyd, 1964.

GREENFIELD, THELMA NELSON. "The Clothing Motif in *King Lear.*" *Shakespeare Quarterly,* 5 (1954), 281–86.

GREG, W. W. *The Shakespeare First Folio.* Oxford: Oxford Univ. Press, 1955.

GRANVILLE-BARKER, HARLEY. *Prefaces to Shakespeare.* 2 vols. Princeton: Princeton Univ. Press, 1947.

HARBAGE, ALFRED. *Shakespeare and the Rival Traditions.* New York: Columbia Univ. Press, 1952.

HARRISON, G. B. *Shakespeare's Tragedies.* London: Routledge and Kegan Paul, 1951.

HAZLITT, WILLIAM. *The Complete Works of William Hazlitt.* London: J. M. Dent and Sons, 1930.

HEILMAN, ROBERT B. *This Great Stage: Image and Structure in "King Lear."* Baton Rouge, La.: Louisiana State Univ. Press, 1948.

HINMAN, CHARLTON. "Introduction to *Timon of Athens.*" Baltimore: Penguin, The Pelican Shakespeare edition, 1964.

HOLLAND, NORMAN. *The Shakespearean Imagination.* New York: Macmillan, 1964.

HOLLOWAY, JOHN. *The Story of the Night: Studies in Shakespeare's Major Tragedies.* London: Kegan Paul, 1961.

HONIG, EDWIN. *Dark Conceit: The Making of Allegory.* Evanson, Ill.: Univ. of Illinois Press, 1959.

HONIGMANN, E. A. J. "*Timon of Athens.*" *Shakespeare Quarterly,* 12 (1961), 3–20.

JAFFA, HARRY V. "The Limits of Politics: An Interpretation of *King Lear,* Act I, Scene I." *American Political Science Review,* 51 (1957), 405–27.

JAMES, D. G. *The Dream of Learning: An Essay on "The Advancement of Learning," "Hamlet" and "King Lear."* Oxford: Oxford Univ. Press, 1951.

JOHNSON, SAMUEL. *Johnson on Shakespeare.* Ed. Walter Raleigh. London: Oxford Univ. Press, 1952.

JONES, ERNEST. *Hamlet and Oedipus.* New York: W. W. Norton, 1949.

JORGENSEN, PAUL A. "A Deed Without a Name." *Pacific Coast Studies in Shakespeare.* Ed. Waldo F. McNeir and Thelma N. Greenfield. Eugene, Ore.: Univ. of Oregon Press, 1966, 190–98.

———. *Lear's Self-Discovery.* Berkeley: Univ. of California Press, 1966.

KANTOROWICZ, ERNST. *The King's Two Bodies.* Princeton: Princeton Univ. Press, 1957.

KAUFMANN, R. J. " 'Ceremonies for Chaos': The Status of *Troilus and Cressida.*" ELH, 23 (1965), 139–59.

KERMODE, FRANK. "The Banquet of Sense." *Bulletin of the John Rylands Library,* 44 (1961), 68–99.

———. *The Sense of an Ending: Studies in the Theory of Fiction.* New York: Oxford Univ. Press, 1967.

KERNAN, ALVIN B. *The Cankered Muse: Satire of the English Renaissance.* New Haven: Yale Univ. Press, 1959.

———. "Formalism and Realism in Elizabethan Drama: The Miracles in *King Lear.*" *Renaissance Drama,* 9 (1966), 59–66.

KIMBROUGH, ROBERT. *Shakespeare's "Troilus and Cressida" and Its Setting.* Cambridge, Mass.: Harvard Univ. Press, 1964.

KIRSCHBAUM, LEO. *Character and Characterization in Shakespeare.* Detroit, Mich.: Wayne State Univ. Press, 1962.

KNIGHT, G. WILSON. *The Wheel of Fire: Interpretations of Shakespearian Tragedy.* London: Methuen, 1930, reprinted, 1949.

KNIGHTS, L. C. "The Ambiguity of *Measure for Measure.*" *Scrutiny,* 10 (1942), 229–38.

———. *Some Shakespearean Themes and An Approach to "Hamlet."* Stanford, Calif.: Stanford Univ. Press, 1966.

KOLVE, V. A. "The Modernity of *Lear.*" *Pacific Coast Studies in Shakespeare.* Ed. Waldo F. McNeir and Thelma N. Greenfield. Eugene, Ore.: Univ. of Oregon Press, 1966, 173–89.

KOTT, JAN. *Shakespeare, Our Contemporary.* Trans. Boselaw Taborski. Garden City, N. Y.: Doubleday, 1964.

KRIEGER, MURRAY. *The Tragic Vision: Variations on a Theme in Literary Interpretation.* Chicago: Univ. of Chicago Press, 1960.

LAMB, CHARLES. *The Complete Works in Prose and Verse of Charles Lamb.* London: Chatto and Windus, 1875.

LAWLOR, JOHN. "*Romeo and Juliet.*" *Early Shakespeare.* Ed. John Russell Brown and Bernard Harris. New York: Schocken Books, 1966.

LAWRENCE, W. W. *Shakespeare's Problem Comedies.* New York: Macmillan, 1931.

LEAVIS, F. R. "The Greatness of *Measure for Measure.*" *Scrutiny,* 10 (1942), 241–50.

LEECH, CLIFFORD. "Ephesus, Troy, Athens: Shakespeare's Use of Locality." *Stratford Papers on Shakespeare,* 47 (1964), 151–69.

LEVIN, HARRY. "The Heights and the Depths: A Scene from *King Lear,*" *More Talking of Shakespeare.* Ed. J. Garrett. London: Longmans, Green, 1959.

LEVIN, RICHARD. "The Unity of Elizabethan Multiple-Plot Drama." *ELH,* 34 (1968), 423–46.

LOTHIAN, JOHN M. "*King Lear*": *A Tragic Reading of Life.* Toronto: Clarke, Irwin, 1949.

LOVEJOY, A. *The Great Chain of Being: A Study of the History of an Idea.* Cambridge, Mass.: Harvard Univ. Press, 1936.

MACK, MAYNARD. "The Jacobean Shakespeare: Some Observations on the Construction of the Tragedies." *Jacobean Theatre.* Ed. John Russell Brown and Bernard Harris. London: Edward Arnold, 1960.

————. *"King Lear" in Our Time.* Berkeley: Univ. of California Press, 1965.

MACLEAN, NORMAN. "Episode, Scene, Speech and Word: The Madness of Lear." *Critics and Criticism.* Ed. R. S. Crane. Chicago: Univ. of Chicago Press, 1952.

MAHOOD, M. M. *Shakespeare's Wordplay.* London: Methuen, 1957.

MAROWITZ, CHARLES. *"Lear* Log" *Tulane Drama Review,* 8 (1963), 103–21.

MARSH, DERICK, R. C. "Interpretation and Misinterpretation: the Problems of *Troilus and Cressida." Shakespeare Studies,* 1 (1965), 182–97.

MATTHIESSEN, F. O. *American Renaissance: Art and Expression in the Age of Emerson and Whitman.* London: Oxford Univ. Press, 1941.

MAXWELL, J. C. *"Timon of Athens." Scrutiny,* 15 (1948), 194–208.

MCALINDON, T. "Language, Style, and Meaning in *Troilus and Cressida." PMLA,* 84 (1969), 29–43.

MCCANLES, MICHAEL. "The Dialectic of Transcendence in Shakespeare's *Coriolanus." PMLA,* 72 (1967), 44–53.

MCFARLAND, THOMAS. *Tragic Meanings in Shakespeare.* New York: Random House, 1966.

MCLUHAN, MARSHALL. *The Gutenberg Galaxy: The Making of Typographic Man.* Toronto: Univ. of Toronto Press, 1962.

————. *Through the Vanishing Point: Space in Poetry and Painting.* New York: Harper and Row, 1968.

MCNEIR, WALDO. "The Staging of the Dover Cliff Scene in *King Lear." Studies in English Renaissance Literature.* Baton Rouge: Louisiana State Univ. Press, 1962, 87–104.

MELVILLE, HERMAN. "Hawthorne and His Mosses." *The Shock of Recognition.* Ed. Edmund Wilson. 2 vols. New York: Grosset & Dunlap, 1943.

MERCHANT, W. M. *"Timon* and the Conceit of Art." *Shakespeare Quarterly,* 6 (1955), 249–57.

MICHEL, LAURENCE. *The Thing Contained: Theory of the Tragic.* Bloomington, Ind.: Indiana Univ. Press, 1970.

MINCOFF, MARCO. *"Measure for Measure*: A Question of Approach." *Shakespeare Studies,* 2 (1966), 141–52.

MURRY, J. MIDDLETON. *Shakespeare.* London: Jonathan Cape, 1936.

NAHM, MILTON C. *Genius and Creativity: An Essay in the History of Ideas.* Baltimore: The Johns Hopkins Press, 1956.

NASSER, EUGENE PAUL. *The Rape of Cinderella.* Bloomington, Ind.: Indiana Univ. Press, 1970.

NICOLL, ALLARDYCE. *Studies in Shakespeare.* London, 1927.

NIETZSCHE, FRIEDRICH. *The Birth of Tragedy.* Trans. Francis Golffing. New York: Doubleday, 1956.

NOWOTTNY, WINIFRED M. T. "Acts IV and V of *Timon of Athens." Shakespeare Quarterly,* 10 (1959), 493–97.

————. "Lear's Questions." *Shakespeare Survey,* 10 (1957), 90–97.

————. "Some Aspects of the Style of *King Lear.*" *Shakespeare Survey,* 13 (1960), 49–57.

OLSON, CHARLES. *Call Me Ishmael.* San Francisco: City Light Books, 1947.

OLSON, ELDER. *Tragedy and the Theory of Drama.* Detroit, Mich.: Wayne State Univ. Press, 1961.

ORNSTEIN, ROBERT. "Historical Criticism and the Interpretation of Shakespeare." *Shakespeare Quarterly,* 10 (1959), 3–9.

PECKHAM, MORSE. *Man's Rage for Chaos; Biology, Behavior, and the Arts.* New York: Schocken Books, 1965.

PETTET, E. C. *Shakespeare and the Romance Tradition.* London: Staples Press, 1949.

————. "*Timon of Athens*: The Disruption of Feudal Morality." RES, 23 (1947), 321–36.

PRICE, H. T. "The Authorship of *Titus Andronicus.*" JEGP, 42 (1943), 55–81.

QUILLER-COUCH, ARTHUR. "Introduction" to *Measure for Measure.* Cambridge: Cambridge Univ. Press, 1922.

RABKIN, NORMAN. "The Double Plot: Notes on the History of a Convention." *Renaissance Drama,* 7 (1964), 55–69.

————. *Shakespeare and the Common Understanding.* New York: The Free Press, 1967.

RAMSEY, JEROLD W. "Timon's Imitation of Christ." *Shakespeare Studies,* 2 (1966), 162–73.

RIGHTER, ANNE. *Shakespeare and the Idea of the Play.* London: Chatto and Windus, 1962.

ROSENBERG, JOHN D. "King Lear and his Comforters." EIC, 16 (1966), 135–46.

ROSSITER, A. P. *Angel With Horns, and Other Shakespearean Lectures.* New York: Theatre Arts, 1961.

SEWELL, ARTHUR. *Character and Society in Shakespeare.* Oxford: Oxford Univ. Press, 1951.

SHAKESPEARE, WILLIAM. *The Complete Works of Shakespeare.* Ed. Hardin Craig. Chicago: Scott, Foresman, 1951.

————. *William Shakespeare: The Complete Works.* Gen. Ed. Alfred Harbage. Baltimore, Md.: Penguin Books, 1969.

————. *William Shakespeare: The Complete Works.* Ed. Charles Jasper Sisson. New York: Harper and Row, 1953.

————. *King Lear.* Ed. Kenneth Muir. Cambridge, Mass.: Harvard Univ. Press, The New Arden Shakespeare, 1952.

————. *Measure for Measure.* Ed. J. W. Lever. Cambridge, Mass.: Harvard Univ. Press, The New Arden Shakespeare, 1965.

———. *Timon of Athens.* Ed. H. J. Oliver. Cambridge, Mass.: Harvard Univ. Press, The New Arden Shakespeare, 1959.

———. *Titus Andronicus.* Ed. J. C. Maxwell. Cambridge, Mass.: Harvard Univ. Press, The New Arden Shakespeare, 1953.

SIEGEL, PAUL N. *Shakespearean Tragedy and the Elizabethan Compromise.* New York: New York Univ. Press, 1957.

SMITH, MARION B. *Dualities in Shakespeare.* Toronto: Univ. of Toronto Press, 1966.

SONTAG, SUSAN. *Styles of Radical Will.* New York: Dell, Delta Books, 1970.

SPENCER, CHRISTOPHER, ed. *Five Restoration Adaptations of Shakespeare.* Urbana, Ill.: Univ. of Illinois Press, 1965.

SPENCER, TERENCE. "Shakespeare Learns the Value of Money: The Dramatist at Work on *Timon of Athens.*" *Shakespeare Survey,* 6 (1953), 75–78.

SPENCER, THEODORE. *Shakespeare and the Nature of Man.* New York: Macmillan, 1949.

SPURGEON, CAROLINE F. E. *Shakespeare's Imagery and What It Tells Us.* Cambridge: Cambridge Univ. Press, 1935, reprinted 1965.

STAMPFER, JUDAH. "The Catharsis of *King Lear.*" *Shakespeare Survey,* 13. Cambridge: Cambridge Univ. Press, 1960.

STAUFFER, DONALD A. *Shakespeare's World of Images: The Development of His Moral Ideas.* New York: W. W. Norton, 1949.

STEINER, GEORGE. *Language and Silence: Essays on Language, Literature and the Inhuman.* New York: Atheneum, 1967.

STEVENSON, DAVID L. *The Achievement of Shakespeare's "Measure for Measure."* Ithaca, N. Y.: Cornell Univ. Press, 1966.

STEWART, J. I. M. *Character and Motive in Shakespeare.* London: Longmans, Green, 1949.

TALBERT, E. W. *Elizabethan Drama and Shakespeare's Early Plays.* Chapel Hill, N. C.: Univ. of North Carolina Press, 1963.

THOMSON, J. A. K. *Shakespeare and the Classics.* London: George Allen & Unwin, 1952.

TILLYARD, E. M. W. *The Elizabethan World Picture.* London: Chatto & Windus, 1943.

———. *Shakespeare's Problem Plays.* London: Chatto & Windus, 1950.

TRAVERSI, DEREK A. *An Approach to Shakespeare.* Garden City: N. Y.: 1956.

VAN DOREN, MARK. *Shakespeare.* New York: Henry Holt, 1939.

WAITH, EUGENE. "The Metamorphosis of Violence in *Titus Andronicus.*" *Shakespeare Survey,* 10 (1957), 39–49.

WARE, MALCOLM. " 'Smoke and Luke-Warm Water': A Note on *Timon of Athens.*" *Anglia,* 82 (1964), 342–44.

WATKINS, W. C. B. *Shakespeare and Spenser*. Princeton: Princeton Univ. Press, 1950.

WEBSTER, MARGARET. *Shakespeare Today*. London: J. M. Dent & Sons, 1957.

WEIL, HERBERT JR. "Form and Contexts in *Measure for Measure*." *Critical Quarterly*, 12 (1970), 55–72.

———. "The Options of the Audience: Theory and Practice in Peter Brooks' *Measure for Measure*." *Shakespeare Survey*, 25 (1972), 27–35.

WELSFORD, ENID. *The Fool: His Social and Literary History*. London: Faber and Faber, 1935.

WHITAKER, VIGIL K. *The Seventeenth Century*. New York: 1951.

WILLIAMS, G. W. "The Poetry of the Storm in *King Lear*." *Shakespeare Quarterly*, 2 (1951), 57–71.

WILSON, HAROLD S. *On the Design of Shakespearian Tragedy*. Toronto: Univ. of Toronto Press, 1957.

Index

159